Educating the Phoenix

Praise for *Educating the Phoenix*

As you read this book, you'll marvel at the unexpected valor from people we look past every day—school "lunch ladies," maintenance personnel, school administrators, bus drivers, and, of course, teachers –ordinary citizens who both followed through on their schools' exceptional safety policies and took heroic initiative when scripted evacuation plans were ineffective or inadequate. Esping and Mercer capture and highlight human ingenuity and self-sacrifice demonstrated on November 8, 2018 in Paradise, California, in ways that renew my hope in the capacity of ordinary American people to do the right thing, with courage, when called upon to act.

—*Frank N. Thomas*, **Emeritus Professor of Counseling and Counselor Education, Texas Christian University, USA**

This book is a powerful testament to the resilience of the human spirit. It chronicles the extraordinary efforts of the Paradise Unified School District to rebuild their community after the devastating Camp Fire. The story of how they persevered, innovated, and ultimately triumphed is both inspiring and informative. This book is a must-read for anyone interested in education, disaster recovery, or the power of human connection.

—*Trinette Marquis*, **APR Executive Director, California School Public Relations Association, USA**

As the former Mayor and another who lost everything in the Camp Fire, I watched our teachers and students come together to heal our community. The strength of our school system is one of the biggest reasons new families are moving to our town as we rebuild our community. Dr. Esping and Ms. Mercer's book, *Educating the Phoenix: Rescuing Children, Reuniting Families and Saving a School District after the 2018 Paradise, California Camp Fire* is a true and accurate retelling of how the PUSD saved our town.

—*Steve "Woody" Culleton*, **Former Mayor of Paradise, California, USA**

The Paradise Unified School District (PUSD) educational leaders demonstrated remarkable resilience in the aftermath of the Camp Fire, showcasing unwavering dedication to rebuilding the community's educational system despite the challenges they faced. We can recount the first hours of the fire and think how remarkable it was that no student was harmed in the evacuation, no easy feat when you have fire burning all around you and only one, jammed up, way out. Where I would note their true strength to be found was in the weeks and months after that, when they had to find students and families, find facilities, find hope, all in the name of restoring "normalcy" back in the lives of their students and staff after such a tragedy. The innovative ways in which they did whatever it would take to get familiar faces back in a classroom, and heal through learning, together, is a story for the history books. *Educating the Phoenix* shows how these school leaders never gave up even though that would have been easier; never gave up when they were both personally and professionally impacted, because they could see the gleam of hope through dark smoke clouds, to focus on rebuilding Paradise.

—Kindra Britt, **Former Deputy Superintendent of Communications and Marketing for the California Department of Education, USA**

I would like to congratulate and thank Dr. Amber Esping for writing this book about our district's remarkable journey as we navigated this unprecedented environmental and human disaster. Her book clearly illustrates many of the actions we undertook, words of wisdom we learned along the way, a bit of advice, and our unrelenting commitment, resiliency, and love for our school district, employees, students, families, and community. Dr. Esping's book is a must-read for district leadership and educational communities as they plan and/or negotiate their way through any disaster that can and will occur at any time to anyone, even a small thriving school district that survived the largest California wildfire to date.

—Michelle John O'Neal, **Former Superintendent of the Paradise Unified School District, USA**

Sometimes a crisis is so widespread that every part of a community is decimated in short order. Some—including COVID-19, Hurricanes Ian and Sandy, the Joplin and Moore tornadoes, and the Camp Fire—are crises of massive magnitude, exceedingly complex and seemingly intractable at every turn. But as these authors show, nothing is intractable in the face of the human spirit and resolve. *Educating the Phoenix* is a testimony to the power of relationships imbued with sense of purpose. The book is both stunning storytelling and a helpful roadmap to thinking through how educational systems can prepare and persevere. How do communications reroute? How are human needs recognized and met? How can families, students, and educators recover and thrive in the aftermath of such devastation? In the vein of *Children of Katrina*, *Educating the Phoenix* shows a path forward, fueled by hope and resilience. In a time where educators are so often critiqued mercilessly, it's important to record stories like the one of Paradise USD personnel, who were nothing short of heroes in response to the Camp Fire. Even in the face of great personal risk, the teachers, staff, and leaders of PUSD did what needed to be done to keep kids safe and, after the Fire, to help them heal and thrive.

—Jo Beth Jimerson, **Professor, William L. and Betty F. Adams Chair of Education, Texas Christian University, Texas USA**

Educating the Phoenix is an amazing deep dive into the dedicated heroes of Paradise Unified School District. So many of us were displaced, living in unfamiliar places, wearing unfamiliar clothes, shaken with fear and uncertainty. This book tells the story of how dedicated individuals came together to restore some form of normalcy to the young people of our community... This is the story of how in a time of grief and fear the people of Paradise Unified showed their true character with generosity and love.

—*Kevin S. McKay*, **Former School Bus Driver Paradise Unified School District; Educator, Chico Unified School District (Portrayed by Matthew McConaughey in the 2025 film,** *The Lost Bus*)**, USA**

Psychological Perspectives on Contemporary Educational Issues

Series Editor
Jonathan Plucker

For over 100 years, psychology has contributed to our understanding of education. These contributions have led to advances in instruction, assessment, student learning, creativity, talent development, and education policy, among many other areas. The *Psychological Perspectives on Contemporary Educational Issues* series provides a venue for scholars to examine important, contemporary issues within education from a psychological perspective, with a goal of proposing new ways to consider, and potentially address, these key issues. Proposals that use the lens of psychology to provide new insights about vexing problems within both formal and informal education are especially encouraged.

Topics of interest include psychological theories applied to practice; psychological perspectives on both the process and goals of education policy; advances in the use of technology to promote and enhance student learning; talent development, creativity, and intelligence; affective outcomes of education; application of sociocultural and emerging theoretical perspectives to learning and instruction; and explorations of how psychological research on education can be strengthened.

OTHER TITLES IN THE SERIES

Exploding the Castle: Rethinking How Video Games & Game Mechanics Can Shape the Future of Education (2017)
Edited by Michael F. Young and Stephen T. Slota.

Instructional Strategies for Improving Students' Learning (2012)
Edited by Jerry S. Carlson and Joel R. Levin.

The No Child Left Behind Legislation (2005)
Edited by Jerry S. Carlson and Joel R. Levin.

Educating the Phoenix

Rescuing Children, Reuniting Families, and Saving a School District After the 2018 Paradise, California Camp Fire

Amber Esping

and

Jess Mercer

United Kingdom – North America – Japan
India – Malaysia – China

Emerald Publishing Limited
Emerald Publishing, Floor 5, Northspring, 21-23 Wellington Street, Leeds LS1 4DL

First edition 2026

Copyright © 2026 by Emerald Publishing Limited.
All rights of reproduction in any form reserved.

Cover photo: Image courtesy of MediaNews Group/The Mercury News via Getty Images

Reprints and permissions service
Contact: www.copyright.com

No part of this book may be reproduced, stored in a retrieval system, transmitted in any form or by any means electronic, mechanical, photocopying, recording or otherwise without either the prior written permission of the publisher or a licence permitting restricted copying issued in the UK by The Copyright Licensing Agency and in the USA by The Copyright Clearance Center. Any opinions expressed in the chapters are those of the authors. Whilst Emerald makes every effort to ensure the quality and accuracy of its content, Emerald makes no representation implied or otherwise, as to the chapters' suitability and application and disclaims any warranties, express or implied, to their use.

British Library Cataloguing in Publication Data
A catalogue record for this book is available from the British Library

ISBN: 978-1-80592-430-2 (Print hardback)
ISBN: 978-1-80592-432-6 (Print paperback)
ISBN: 978-1-80592-429-6 (Ebook)
ISBN: 978-1-80592-431-9 (EPUB)

Typeset by TNQ Tech
Cover design by TNQ Tech

Dedicated to the People of the Paradise Unified School District

CONTENTS

About the Authors xiii

Foreword xv

Acknowledgments xvii

1 Introduction 1

2 Every Kid Made It 15

3 Reuniting Parents and Children 43

4 Keeping the Students Together 49

5 The School in the Hardware Store 71

6 Even Heroes Are Human 83

7 Embracing Radical Empathy 103

8 Phoenix Rising 113

Epilogue 119

Appendix A: Advice From Our Experts 127

Appendix B: Selected Resources 135

ABOUT THE AUTHORS

Amber Esping, Ph.D. is an associate professor of Educational Psychology at Texas Christian University in Fort Worth, Texas, USA. In many of her previous publications, Amber wrote about researchers who have built meaningful careers around studying social phenomena related to their own personal adversity (e.g. her 2018 book, *Epistemology, Ethics, and Meaning in Unusually-Personal Scholarship*). The faculty members she met through this work view themselves as "wounded healers." For them, writing and teaching provides access to both a successful scholarly career and a personal pathway through challenge. Writing *Educating the Phoenix* provided an opportunity to put into practice what she has learned from this work; Amber's parents and brother escaped Paradise by driving through the Fire with only the clothes they were wearing, some important financial documents, and three pets. Fortunately, they were able to rebuild and move back to Esping Way just ahead of the third anniversary of the Fire. Amber's nephew Jacob graduated from Paradise High School 62 years after her Dad did, in 2021. Amber lives in Texas, and has two sons and a daughter with her husband, Thomas. This is her fourth book.

Jess Mercer is a Paradise, California, USA community artist and an expert on trauma-informed art education. She is the founder of Butte County Art on Wheels, a community-oriented mobile therapeutic art studio and She has been deeply rooted in Paradise since she moved to the town with her father at age fifteen, but she came to national prominence with the creation of the *Ridge Key Phoenix*, a striking 800-pound monument created from more than 18,000 keys that once opened the doors to homes, schools, businesses, cars and places of worship in Paradise. She has been featured in media ranging from CNN and NPR to the BBC, but more meaningful for her are the numerous local awards, among them the *Key to the Town of Paradise* (the first recipient of this honor since the town was incorporated in 1979), and the Paradise Unified School District *Caring Heart Award*, both in 2019. She created and directs Camp Fire survivor school programs including "Tap-Pen, Tap-Out," "15 in 15 Murals," and the "Balanced Brain Project," a 36-week, trauma-informed therapeutic art program focusing on trauma and self-awareness in students impacted by the Camp Fire and other adverse childhood experiences. She is the founder of Butte County Art on Wheels, a community-oriented mobile therapeutic art studio. Jess's parents lost their home in the Camp Fire, which also destroyed the art studio she shared with her father. Jess currently lives in the neighboring city of Chico with her wife, Ashley.

FOREWORD

As the former Superintendent for Paradise Unified School District, I was humbled and honored when asked to write the Foreword for this inspiring story. As I read each chapter of *Educating the Phoenix: Rescuing Children, Reuniting Families and Saving a School District after the 2018 Paradise, California Camp Fire,* I was brought back to a time of hard work surrounded by many visionary individuals. I remembered the tears, laughter, innovation, and the joy of working side by side with a brilliant team. Each of us carried our own trauma, and we realized we needed one another to keep doing our important work. I hope when you have completed this book you are able to come away with the belief that by working together and holding each other up, you can overcome what is thought by many to be unattainable.

I would like to congratulate and thank Dr. Amber Esping for writing this book about our district's remarkable journey as we navigated this unprecedented environmental and human disaster. Her book clearly illustrates many of the actions we undertook, words of wisdom we learned along the way, a bit of advice, and our unrelenting commitment, resiliency, and love for our school district, employees, students, families, and community.

Dr. Esping's book is a must read for district leadership and educational communities as they plan and/or negotiate their way through any disaster that can and will occur at any time to anyone, even a small thriving school district that survived the largest California wild fire to date.

Michelle John O'Neal, Retired Superintendent,
Paradise Unified School District, USA

ACKNOWLEDGMENTS

Our deepest thanks to the Paradise Unified School District employees who agreed to be represented by name in this book: Tanya Harter, Larry Johnson, Dena Kapsalis, Reiner Light, David McCready, Michelle John O'Neal, Tracy Parks, Chris Rinesmith, Linda Shields, Cynthia Smith, Victoria Steindorf, Tom Taylor, Jacob Timm, and Angie Van Blaricom.

We are also indebted to everyone else who lived this story but who is not named in these pages. We hope this book honors your anonymous contributions to your town and its children. We know many teachers, administrators, and PUSD staff who are reading this book personally saved students' lives on November 8, 2018. We also know that, seven years on, many of you are still doing this in smaller but significant ways every day. Bless you and thank you.

We wish to acknowledge our family members who experienced the Fire first-hand: Gilbert Esping, Mary Esping, Michael Esping, and Ashley Mercer.

Jess Mercer would like to thank the thousands of strangers in Paradise who welcomed and trusted her offers of help.

We are grateful to the volunteers at the Gold Nugget Museum in Paradise who assisted in creating the Resource list at the end of this book.

Two Texas Christian University master's students, Noortje Hermanns and Josie Ferrante, provided indispensable support throughout this project. Noortje gathered and summarized media accounts of the Camp Fire, helped conduct two interviews, and visited Paradise for the Third Anniversary Community Unifying Event. Josie transcribed many of our interviews and assisted with obtaining permission to use specific photographs.

Amber would like to thank her Texas family, who supported her in so many ways during the writing of this book–Thomas, Donna, Dylan, Khalil, and Merideth—and also Bobby and Kelli Spencer, who offered necessary support towards the end of the project.

A huge thank you to Jonathan Plucker, our Series Editor at Emerald (and longtime supporter in so many ways), and Cathy Sellars, Emerald Publishing Operations Editor.

We have no known conflicts of interest to disclose. We did not receive financial support for this book. Correspondence concerning this book should be addressed to Amber Esping, Department of Counseling, Societal Change, and Inquiry, Texas Christian University, TCU Box 297900, Fort Worth, TX, 76129.

CHAPTER 1

INTRODUCTION

> *May you find Paradise to be all its name implies*
> —Road sign as you enter the town of Paradise, California

Nearly four weeks after the devastating November 8, 2018 Camp Fire obliterated the town of Paradise, California, I (Amber) found myself spending yet another late night obsessively scrolling social media for information. The home my elderly parents shared with my brother was one of the nearly 14,000 homes destroyed (Boghani, 2019). Since it had been hard for my family to access updates from their temporary berths at the Oroville Nazarene Church, the Yuba City Red Cross shelter, and eventually a hotel room two hours from Paradise, I was trying to relay necessary information from my own home in Texas. The 3-minute video currently on my screen had been uploaded to the Town of Paradise Facebook page earlier that day. The speaker was Matt Gates, Public Information Officer for the Town. Dressed casually in a long-sleeved plaid shirt and jeans, he stood in front of a devastated house. A brick chimney was the last waypost signifying that this had once been a family home, and it was surrounded on all sides by indecipherable piles of char. It was disorienting, impossible for my brain to create order out of the scene.

Gates was offering information for Paradise residents who were impatiently awaiting the reopening of evacuation zones. The town was a black, fuliginous wasteland and an attractive target for looters, yes, but it was also saturated with toxic chemicals and nearly 100,000 huge, unstable, "hazard trees" that could fall at any time (Associated Press, 2019; Curwen & Serna, 2018). For these reasons the perimeter of the Fire scar around Paradise and the neighboring communities was locked down and patrolled 24/7 by a contingent of the US Army National Guard. This provisional reopening of Paradise at the checkpoint would be the residents' first opportunity since their escape to see with their own eyes what, if anything, remained of their homes, businesses, schools, and places of worship. "You will be going through a checkpoint where they will be issuing some personal protective gear," Gates said in the video.

> I'm gonna demonstrate how that protective gear works. Included in there, there's gonna be a full-body Tyvek® suit, some rubber gloves, an N95 mask, and some information that you should go over before you begin to go through the remains of your property.

The video cuts here, and then Gates goes on. "We want to remind everyone that when you return home," he gestures to the debris behind him, "there are a lot of hazards that you'll want to be aware of." He turns away again, and for the first time the cadence of his speech accelerates. His shoulders drop, signaling resignation to a difficult situation.

"Um…behind me is my house."

The moment passes in an instant, and he's back to giving advice about how to safely sift through rubble. What a crushing example of quiet, unflashy heroism, I thought, this man just doing his job so competently among the ruins of his family home. It was not *a* house. It was *his* house.

By the time I saw Gates's video I was already familiar with many more dazzling examples of courage—ubiquitous accounts of firefighters and police driving and even running in preternatural late-morning darkness toward the danger (see Honea, 2018 for a dramatic video), and of medical personnel who stayed with critically ill patients while nine campus buildings, the main hospital, and one of the two ambulances en route to their location, burned around them (Gabbert, 2019). I had also begun hearing about parents, teachers, bus drivers, and other Paradise Unified School District (PUSD) employees who shepherded thousands of children and teens to safety through and between walls of flame that were, quite literally, melting the metal on the vehicles they were driving (Gee & Anguiano, 2021; Villareal, 2018). Some of these rescuers sang songs for the children and feigned confidence. Others prayed for either safe deliverance or a quick death. Some teachers who stayed with 22 elementary children escaping by bus prayed that the "smoke would kill them first" (Johnson, 2021, p. 166). One female school employee I spoke with rescued four elementary school students with one other adult in her personal car. When it looked like the Fire was set to overtake them, she contemplated whether she possessed the physical and emotional capacity to render the children unconscious quickly:

> This was my hardest moment. 10:26 in the morning. It's pitch black. There's power poles and telephone poles that were on Fire. And I'm driving…, and I had

this thought of if that falls, we're trapped. And I'm going, "how do you knock somebody out? If those kids are in the car, like are we gonna die of asphyxiation first? Or are we gonna burn? Like can I hit these kids so I can knock them out?" Because I had a second grader, a third grader, and two fourth graders.

I had no doubt that many of these heroes were watching Gates's video with me, and that by now they also already knew, intellectually if not yet viscerally, that they had no home or friend's home or favorite store or church or school or pets to come back to once the borders opened. These people, displaced and traumatized, were about to save Paradise's children once again.

THE MAGNITUDE OF THE DAMAGE

When school started on November 8, 2018 the PUSD boasted a thriving network of 11 campuses housing 3,401 students and 390 full-time employees (D. McCready, personal communication, February 3, 2023). Four hours later, three schools were reduced to ash and all PUSD power, communications and maintenance infrastructures were wiped out. The foodservice warehouse and offices were gone. The transportation office was gone. The bus yard and its compressed natural gas filling station were damaged (J. Timm, personal communication, November 5, 2021). Seventeen buses were damaged or reduced to melted, sooty shells (M. John O'Neal, personal communication, October 9, 2021). The remaining eight campuses were in various states of ruin, from smoke damage only (one school and the District Office) to partially or mostly destroyed (seven schools) (J. Timm, personal communication, November 5, 2021). Much of the damage was irreparable (See Table 1.1). The students and teachers were scattered in a diaspora that spanned the US and internationally (See Figure 1.1). Those who remained local bunked in tents, cars,

TABLE 1.1 Paradise Unified School District Status After the Camp Fire	
Elementary Schools	
Cedarwood	Smoke damage only
Pine Ridge	One portable destroyed, two damaged; gym electrical panel and siding damaged
Ponderosa	Multipurpose room damaged beyond repair; administration building damaged beyond repair; six Kindergarten portable classrooms destroyed; two portable classroom buildings were destroyed at the south end of campus (District Nurse and Music room); Building F at the south end of campus was damaged at the overhang from trees that were just feet away
Paradise	Entire site destroyed

(Continued)

TABLE 1.1 Paradise Unified School District Status After the Camp Fire (continued)

Junior High Schools	
Paradise Intermediate School	One one-room stick built structure destroyed
Evergreen Sixth-Grade	Four portable classrooms destroyed; one portable office/library destroyed; one portable restroom destroyed
Creekside Sixth-Grade	Four portable classrooms destroyed; one portable restroom destroyed
High Schools	
Paradise High School	Five portable classrooms were destroyed at the north end of campus; auto shop roof was damaged; athletic training room was damaged; softball field lighting, backstop and scoreboard were destroyed; baseball field scoreboard was destroyed; north end of the running track was severely damaged; septic treatment plant was destroyed; three modular classrooms at the south end of campus had all of the electrical wiring on the exterior destroyed, along with siding and Bard HVAC units; portable classroom at the northeast across the street from PHS destroyed along with its septic system
Ridgeview Continuation High School	All buildings except the shop were destroyed; the shop (which is a metal building) sustained damage to the metal siding on the south side and a wooden overhang over the man door and compressor was destroyed
Other School Types	
Honey Run Academy (servicing students who have an education expulsion order, probation referral, attendance review board referral, or administrative order)	Two portable classrooms and one portable office were destroyed; a house used for storage was destroyed; the septic system was destroyed
Pearson Center Day School (servicing individuals with intellectual and developmental disabilities)	Entire building destroyed, along with a house that was at the north end of the property
Administration and Operations	
Maintenance	Steel maintenance building with storage and offices destroyed; two Quonset huts for maintenance equipment storage/supplies damaged
Food Service	Foodservice warehouse and offices destroyed; three walk-in freezer units destroyed
Transportation Yard	Compressed natural gas bus filling station damaged; bus barn south exterior wall damaged; transportation portable office destroyed; 17 buses and multiple district vehicles destroyed
District Office	Smoke damage only
Power and Communications	Destroyed

Source: Author's own.

Figure 1.1 Camp Fire Survivor Diaspora, based on US Post Office change of address requests. An original digital image courtesy of Peter Hansen.

trailers, shelters, hotels, and in tense and crowded conditions with relatives and friends living outside the burn scar. Indeed, 70% of PUSD's full-time employees lost their homes or were temporarily or permanently displaced due to Fire damage or other hazards (T. Taylor, personal communication, February 3, 2023). Many would never return.

WHAT INFORMATION IS IN THIS BOOK?

The focus of this book is rebuilding an entire school system in the wake of absolute physical devastation and population diaspora from wildfire. On November 8, 2018, 90% of Paradise's population of approximately 26,500 residents left town in about the same time it takes to watch the movie *Gone with the Wind*. It seemed inevitable to many that PUSD would shut down, perhaps permanently, with any remaining students transferring to neighboring school districts. This was what California law required under these circumstances, but this is not what the students or their parents said they wanted. When PUSD leadership visited with families, the message was clear: These children had already lost nearly everything else that was stable their lives, and dispersing them to unfamiliar schools would be another blow. They wanted to be together with their friends and their teachers. Hearing this feedback, Paradise Superintendent Michelle John O'Neal led the charge to keep the PUSD intact. From the County Superintendent level all the way to California Governor Gavin Newsom's office, she implored, "Give me a couple weeks to try and find places to bring kids together because that's what their parents are asking for." She prevailed, and many kids came back—even if they or their parents had to drive hours every day to get to school, and even if they had to go to school in some very unconventional locations. Larry Johnson, who was principal of Paradise Intermediate (relocated to an empty Orchard Supply Hardware (OSH) store in the neighboring city of Chico) described how meaningful this turned out to be:

> The fact that one kid, even one kid, would go to school in a hardware store instead of a school that was probably much easier to get to, it's just remarkable. The fact that so many kids reunited and came back. And parents would literally drive from hours away just to get their kids to school to be with their teachers and their friends.

As we approach the five-year anniversary of the Camp Fire on November 8, 2023, Paradise Unified is a dynamic, fully functioning district with six beautiful campuses and an e-learning academy. Enrollment is 1,576 students (46% of its pre-Fire value) who are served by 110 full-time teachers (57% of pre-Fire). Now, as before the Fire, many of the students struggle economically (Pre-Fire, Social Security was the main source of income for people in Paradise, and nearly 70% of the student body qualified for free or reduced lunch). There are drugs on the Ridge. Kids get into trouble. Mental health, an important consideration for Paradise schools even before the Camp Fire, is an even more vital area of concern. But despite all the challenges, the Paradise schools have emerged from the ashes as vibrant spaces where an ethic of caring pervades both large-scale decision-making and small, personal interactions. The District describes itself on the California Department of Education accountability website as a "hub for community," a "safe place for families as well as a source of hope in our community," and a resource that is "often looked to as the leading organization in the [town] rebuilding process" (California Department of Education, 2022). Sports are enthusiastically attended. Visual arts thrive. Most important of all, children and teens learn together in classrooms with their teachers and friends. This book tells the remarkable story of how the people of the PUSD made this happen.

Michelle John O'Neal, PUSD Superintendent at the time of the Camp Fire, identified six individuals who were part of the key leadership team during the disaster, its immediate aftermath, and the long process of rebuilding. We were able to interview five of these people: Michelle and her two assistant superintendents, Tom Taylor and David McCready; Dena Kapsalis, Director of Student Services; Jacob Timm, Director of Facilities, Maintenance and Operations; and Reiner Light, Camp Fire Educational Coordinator. The sixth member of this leadership team, PUSD legal counsel, did not participate in the present book. We also called on the wisdom of other essential District personnel, including Paradise Intermediate School Principal Larry Johnson; teachers Cynthia Smith, Tracy Parks, and Victoria Steindorf; bus driver/trainer Chris Rinesmith and bus driver Angie Van Blaricom; Director of Food Services Tanya Harter, and Food Service Site Manager Linda Shields. We supplemented their first-person accounts with deep dives into the Camp Fire news coverage. My coauthor, Jess Mercer, works in Paradise and was present during the Fire and throughout the rebuilding. I visited Paradise several times a year, toured the schools, and attended various commemorations and community celebrations of milestones.

Chapter 2, *Every Kid Made It*, focuses on the actions of PUSD administrators, teachers, bus drivers, food service professionals, and other staff the morning of the Camp Fire. We provide evidence that these individuals collectively saved the lives of thousands of school children on November 8, 2018.

Chapter 3, *Reuniting Parents and Children*, explains how the people of the PUSD, assisted by volunteers from the Church of Jesus Christ of Latter-day Saints, kept the students safe, warm, and fed at the evacuation sites. It also describes Paradise Intermediate School's successful plan for reuniting all PUSD students with their families.

Chapter 4, *Keeping the Students Together* explains how the people of the PUSD fought to keep the District open after the Fire had destroyed nearly all of its schools and left approximately 70% of its employees and nearly all of its students homeless.

Chapter 5, *The School in the Hardware Store*, is a case study of Paradise Intermediate School, which relocated to an empty OSH store in a neighboring city. The teachers transformed the aisles into classrooms. Lunch ladies served meals from the checkstands. Physical education took place in the garden center. This school serves as a beautiful example of commitment, creativity, and community in the wake of disaster.

Chapter 6, *Even Heroes are Human*, describes how the PUSD administrators, teachers and staff supported each other while caring for their students' emotional needs after the Fire. Much of the success in rebuilding the District can be attributed to this ethic of caring.

Chapter 7, *Embracing Radical Empathy*, is coauthor Jess Mercer's first-person account of her trauma-informed art education practice with the PUSD schools. Jess describes her personal experience of the Fire, focusing on how her personal history prepared her to respond to tragedy in such a public way. She also tells the story of how the *Ridge Key Phoenix* came to be. This chapter is unique in that the information has not been filtered through another writer's interpretation, as is the case with our interview-based chapters.

Chapter 8, *Phoenix Rising*, offers a summary of the resilience factors individual PUSD employees were able to draw on while recovering from the Camp Fire.

We close with an Epilogue, where we look back on the Camp Fire recovery and catch up with the PUSD employees introduced in previous chapters. Appendix A offers bulleted advice from each of them. Appendix B lists selected books, websites, and films pertaining to the Camp Fire, Paradise, and the PUSD.

WHO IS THIS BOOK FOR?

We wrote this book for the people of the PUSD, and also for school leaders, teachers, counselors, bus drivers, cafeteria and maintenance staff, paraprofessionals, and others who wish to learn from their extraordinary example. Massive wildfires and other forms of environmental catastrophe are becoming so common that it may be worth planning ahead for your own school district (Smith, 2019; Stanley, 2021). Case in point: On August 8, 2023, one day before Paradise USD celebrated the grand opening of its beautiful new high school campus, the town of Lahaina, in Maui, burned to the ground. The death toll, still uncertain as I write this, has already surpassed the Camp Fire. Paradise is of course reaching out, "from one Paradise to another" to share their unique expertise.

Fire disaster recovery is not the only area where the Paradise USD example can be useful. As I began writing the first draft of this Introduction three years after the Camp Fire, I was simultaneously contemplating how I would connect with my own students in Texas the following day. It was the spring of 2021, and the Covid-19 pandemic was still a major factor in the United States. Vaccines were just starting to roll out, and it had been almost one year since I taught my last in-person class at my university. Since then I had become quite comfortable teaching over Zoom, this supposed "new normal" to which almost every teacher and professor had accommodated. However, that week we were also experiencing an unprecedented snowstorm in North Texas, leaving many of my students without electric power, natural gas, or water. Local Texans had resorted to burning their own furniture, toys, and fences in an attempt to keep warm (Bernard, 2021). Ultimately 246 Texans would die that week from the cold.

That afternoon my university administration offered guidelines for delivering asynchronous instruction and extending assignment deadlines until the power came back on. I was confident that students, teachers, and professors alike would pivot with minimal disruption to learning. We had all learned to be more flexible and patient, and we'd worked hard to gain the wisdom and discernment necessary for navigating logistical challenges to pedagogy with both rigor and kindness. But I also knew that the real experts in flexible, responsive teaching during the hardest and most uncertain of times are the Paradise USD leaders, teachers, and staff. These folks reunited a community of learners after the Fire, and then almost immediately turned their newfound flexibility and wisdom toward navigating COVID-19. We can all use their help right now. And thankfully, despite everything the people of the PUSD have endured, and also because of it, they were willing to share their experiences and insights with Jess Mercer and me.

JESS MERCER

Jess Mercer is the coauthor of this book, but she is also a Paradise institution in herself. Chapter 7 offers Jess's first-person account, but I (Amber) think it is important to frame her contributions briefly here. Jess is a Paradise community artist and expert on trauma-informed art education. Jess has been deeply rooted in Paradise since she moved to the town with her father at age 15, but she came to national prominence with the creation of the *Ridge Key Phoenix*, a striking 800-pound monument created from more than 18,000 keys that once opened the doors to homes, schools, businesses, cars and places of worship in Paradise. The Smithsonian wanted it, but you will only see it in Paradise. The reader can find a photograph of the *Ridge Key Phoenix* in Chapter 7 (Image 7.1).

Jess has been featured in media ranging from CNN and NPR to the BBC, but more meaningful for her are the numerous local awards, among them the *Key to the Town of Paradise* (the first recipient of this honor since the town was incorporated in 1979), and the PUSD *Caring Heart Award*, both in 2019. She created and directs Camp Fire survivor school programs including "Tap-Pen, Tap-Out," "15 in 15 Murals," and the "Balanced Brain Project," a 36-week, trauma-informed therapeutic art program focusing on trauma and self-awareness in students impacted by the Camp Fire and other adverse childhood experiences. She is the founder of Butte County Art on Wheels, a community-oriented mobile therapeutic art studio (Butte County Art on Wheels, n.d.). Jess's parents lost their home in the Camp Fire, which also destroyed the art studio she shared with her father. Her parents remain part of the Paradise diaspora, having settled about 45 minutes away. Jess's dad has only been back to the town twice since the Fire, once to see the unveiling of the *Ridge Key Phoenix*, and once to see the wellness center Jess built for Paradise. Jess currently lives in the neighboring city of Chico with her wife, Ashley.

The goodwill Jess enjoys from her community made this book possible. When this seeming outsider from Texas wanted to speak with school personnel, Jess offered a warm-handoff and a sense of safety and trust. People were willing to talk with me because Jess vouched for me. I owe her a tremendous debt.

AMBER ESPING

As for me (Amber Esping), I am an educational psychology professor living in Texas. My family's roots in Paradise go back to my grandparents. My Dad grew up in town, on a private gravel road named for the family—Esping Way. Dad graduated from Paradise High School in 1959. He eventually left to join the US Army and then the Los Angeles Police Department, but it was always his dream to move back to Paradise. He came home for good in 1999 after he retired. Mom and Dad built a modular home next door to Grandpa's mobile home on Esping Way. My brother, sister, niece and nephew eventually followed. The Camp Fire swept up all the homes and vehicles on Esping Way, along with the town's beloved Gold Nugget Museum just up the road. My family escaped by driving through the Fire, with only the clothes they were wearing, some important financial documents, and three pets. Unlike many in Paradise, they were well-insured and they were able to rebuild and move back just ahead of the third anniversary of the Fire. My nephew Jacob graduated from Paradise High School in 2021, 62 years after my Dad.

A NOTE ON OBJECTIVITY AND LIMITATIONS

There are many in academia who would warn Jess and I not to engage in scholarship with which we have such close personal and painful connections. I understand these epistemological and ethical challenges pretty well, having taken a deep dive into these matters in my 2018 book, *Epistemology, Ethics, and Meaning in Unusually Personal Scholarship* (Esping, 2018). At the time I wrote *Epistemology*, I did not foresee these issues applying so directly to me, but here we are. In past projects I have at times cried with folks, but for the most part I have been able to do my job—to steward other people's stories—from marginal emotional distance. These were not my narratives, but through the trust and generosity of the participants I was invited to translate their experiences for other outsiders. This book is different. Matt Gates and his safety video offer a compelling metaphor here. Figuratively speaking, behind me is my parents' house. Behind Jess Mercer is her parents' house, the private art studio that she shared with her Dad, and the charred remains of about 19,000 other homes, businesses, schools, and places of worship that formed her beloved community (Boghani, 2019). This oral history is arrestingly personal.

This book is massively incomplete. We offer a portrait of the Paradise USD only, which means that we did not write about adjacent towns and unincorporated communities that also suffered near-total destruction. Moreover, this book doesn't claim to be a comprehensive picture of the Paradise schools. We elected to dive deep with a few people rather than reaching out to a larger representation of the hundreds of PUSD teachers, administrators, and staff we might have. This choice speaks to the magnitude of the heroism in Paradise on November 8, 2018. Every compelling personal story in these pages must stand for the others, at least here. PUSD Superintendent Tom Taylor (Assistant Superintendent during the Camp Fire) explained this best when we asked him if he would be willing to "share some important stories" about staff members getting their students out and to safety on the morning of the Fire. Here is what he said:

> You know, it isn't one person that day. Everybody played a part...*so many* people, the majority by far, reacted in such an incredible way that there isn't *one story*. I mean, everybody has a similar story about getting people out, staying with their classroom, calling parents, being sure that the kids are picked up. And it's not just that it's putting kids in your car and getting down the hill the best that you can. It's really that there's *so many*. There's not one story. I think to try to put a single name to a story, when everybody was doing so much. It would discredit some people and I don't want to.

Sacrificing breadth for depth means that many deeply meaningful stories were left out of this book. If you live in Paradise, then you already know that your child's teachers, administrators, counselors, food servers, custodians, bus drivers, administrative personnel, and other support staff are heroes. If you don't live there, then just assume that behind every narrative this book there are many hundreds more just as significant. And with this disclaimer Jess and I humbly submit this book as a tribute to the—and let's boldly dispense with objectivity for a moment—the *absolute freaking miracle* that is the PUSD.

In subsequent chapters "I" and "My" will refer to the first author, Amber Esping. The exception is Chapter 7, "Embracing Radical Empathy," which was authored by Jess Mercer.

All author royalties from the sale of this book benefit Jess's organization, Butte County Art on Wheels.

REFERENCES

Associated Press. (2019, April 19). Fire in Paradise, California, poisoned the water with 'toxic cocktail'. https://www.nbcnews.com/news/us-news/Fire-paradise-california-poisoned-water-toxic-cocktail-n996136

Bernard, M. (2021, February 18). *Burning the furniture and blaming the wind.* Natural Resources Defense Council. https://www.nrdc.org/experts/mitchell-bernard/burning-furniture-and-blaming-wind

Boghani, P. (2019, October 29). *Camp Fire: By the numbers.* Frontline. https://www.pbs.org/wgbh/frontline/article/camp-Fire-by-the-numbers/

Butte County Art on Wheels. (n.d.). https://cds.bcoe.org/Services/Teaching–Learning/Visual-and-Performing-Arts/Orgs/Butte-County-Art-on-Wheels–Jess-Mercer/

California Department of Education. (2022). *Paradise Unified: Conditions and climate.* https://www.caschooldashboard.org/reports/04615310000000/2022/conditions-and-climate

Curwen, T., & Serna, J. (2018, November 20). Thousands of homes incinerated but trees still standing. *Los Angeles Times.* https://www.govtech.com/em/disaster/thousands-of-homes-incinerated-but-trees-still-standing-paradise-Fires-mmonstrous-path.html

Esping, A. (2018). *Epistemology, ethics, and meaning in unusually personal scholarship.* Palgrave.

Gabbert, B. (2019, February 26). Feather River Hospital evacuated 280 patients and staff as Camp Fire approached. https://wildfiretoday.com/feather-river-hospital-evacuated-280-patients-and-staff-as-camp-fire-approached/

Gates, M. (2018, December 3). *With the anticipated re-opening of the evacuation zones approaching soon, we want to remind everyone to take appropriate precautions to mitigate exposure to hazardous materials* [Video]. Facebook. https://fb.watch/gHRJHafyuu/

Gee, A., & Anguiano, D. (2021). *Fire in Paradise: An American tragedy.* WW Norton & Co.

Honea, K. (2018). Body-worn footage of Camp Fire rescue [Video]. KTVU Fox 2 San Francisco. https://youtu.be/XBvJBIapIc8

Johnson, L. (2021). *Paradise: One town's struggle to survive an American wildfire*. Crown.

Mercer, J. (n.d.). Jess Mercer in the news. https://cds.bcoe.org/Services/Teaching–Learning/Visual-and-Performing-Arts/Orgs/Butte-County-Art-on-Wheels–Jess-Mercer/

Smith, A. B. (2019, February 7). *2018's billion-dollar disasters in context*. National Oceanic and Atmospheric Administration. https://www.climate.gov/news-features/blogs/beyond-data/2018s-billion-dollar-disasters-context

Stanley, A. (2021, October 27). The coming age of climate trauma. *The Washington Post Magazine*. https://www.washingtonpost.com/magazine/2021/10/27/camp-fire-ptsd/

Villareal, M. (2018, November 12). California's Camp Fire burned hot enough to melt aluminum in cars. https://www.cbsnews.com/news/californias-camp-Fire-burned-hot-enough-to-melt-aluminum-in-cars/

CHAPTER 2

EVERY KID MADE IT

> *Every kid made it, every staff member made it, which is pretty much a miracle. I mean, the staff, they were incredible, throwing kids in their cars…it was the people who were at the sites that were making the split-second decisions…It goes back to what everybody did at their own site that day, and being sure they were taking care of kids, which is what an educator's job is.*
>
> —Tom Taylor, PUSD Assistant Superintendent during Camp Fire; PUSD Superintendent, 2020–present

Every child got out. No other statement tells the story of the Paradise Unified School District like this one does. It is in itself poetry, the alpha and omega, the gestalt, the mic drop, the *mise en scène* for everything that follows in this book. It is indeed so important a fact that some of the people we interviewed told us that it was the part of the Paradise Unified School District (PUSD) story they had the most difficulty talking about. Very eager and forthright otherwise, there was not much off limits in our interviews. Jess and I agreed early on that we would not ask any direct questions about people's actual escape from the Camp Fire, not wanting to retraumatize anyone in the retelling. We informed everyone of this when recruiting them for the interviews, and again at the start of each interview. Nevertheless, nearly everyone we talked with volunteered aspects of their traumatic experiences on November 8, 2018. There were only two things our participants were hesitant to talk about: (1) Their personal heroism, which we would only hear about during their colleagues' interviews, and (2) the fact that no students or staff died in the fire. The most stoic avoided this last subject, noting that they feared emotion might overwhelm them if they talked about it too directly.

All of the approximately 3,400 students who were present in school or on school buses that day escaped. That is a strong word to use, *escape*, but it is the right one. "Evacuate" doesn't come close to capturing the experience. The Fire started so early in the morning and moved so fast that no one could be fully prepared for what was about to happen. The previous day officials noted the strong winds and parched vegetation, and predicted a very high level of fire risk known as a "Red Flag Warning." This sounds scary, and it is, but this was fairly typical for this part of California, which was in the midst of a shocking and historic drought. Most people had transitioned from thinking in terms of a "fire season" to a more generalized sense of risk year-round. Paradise, in particular, had robust wildfire preparedness and mitigation education programs, many spearheaded by the Paradise Ridge Fire Safe Council. This group of community members was chaired by Phil John, husband to Paradise USD school superintendent Michelle John O'Neal. Phil was well-known for showing up at school and town events dressed as the Council's delightful and fluffy fire safety mascot, "Ready Raccoon."

The Red Flag Warning turned out to be right on target. At approximately 6:30am on November 8, 2018, an utterly neglected, nearly 100-year-old Pacific Gas & Electric (PG&E) powerline sparked in a wooded area just to the northeast of Paradise.[1] The first firefighter arrived 15 minutes later, but the Fire was unreachable by truck. Air attacks were not permitted until 30 minutes after sunrise, and it was still dark. The firefighter radioed his assessment that this small Fire looked like it could become a "major incident" (Epley, 2019). He was right. At its peak it was consuming 80 football fields every minute (Boghani, 2019), burning hot enough to melt the volcanic Paradise soil into metallic slivers, and blister lungs in a single breath (Johnson, 2021, p. 66).

By around 7:00am the Fire had already absorbed ten acres, while 50 mile-per-hour winds continued to prevent tracking or fighting the Fire by air. The Butte County Sheriff's Department ordered the tiny, nearby town of Pulga to evacuate, as a second small town, Concow, caught fire. At 7:59 Paradise began burning. The PUSD schools begin their days between 8:25am and

---

[1] Much has already been written about PG&E's culpability for the Camp Fire. The present book will not address this issue directly, as our focus is the PUSD. We do wish to acknowledge here, however, that PG&E pled guilty to 84 counts of involuntary manslaughter, and has been ordered to pay a multibillion-dollar settlement for repeatedly failing to maintain the power line that caused the Camp Fire. People in Paradise are still very, very angry with PG&E. Many believe this company is responsible for destroying everything they had worked for, for their whole lives, and for killing their loved ones and pets. (The ones who died in the fire, and the many others who people believe died from various fire-related causes-emotional and physical—in the ensuing months and years.) PG&E is not a subject you bring up in Paradise unless you are ready for an impassioned response.

8:40am, so many staff, teachers and students were already in school buses or at their campuses when the flames arrived in town. The schools began evacuating children as first responders and Paradise residents started going door-to-door, waking their neighbors and urging them to *leave, now*. Some PUSD students' parents had already left for work. Without the schools, many of their children would have been home alone.

At 8:03am the Butte County Sherriff's Department issued an evacuation order for the eastern half of Paradise. Trees began to fall, trapping fire crews and residents. People began dying. Children traveled to school in buses, many oblivious. Meanwhile, 911 lines had become overrun with calls reporting raining ash and heavy smoke in Paradise. Dispatcher Carol Ladrini called the California Department of Forestry and Fire Protection ("CAL FIRE") twice, and she was repeatedly assured that Paradise was not under threat. Carol reassured the callers that there is just "a lot of smoke right now." She finally received the evacuation notice 18 minutes after the fire crossed into Paradise (Taddonio, 2019). This was very much too late.

By 8:15 Feather River Hospital in Paradise began burning and the staff began evacuating patients. At 8:41 the Butte County Sherriff's office issued further evacuation orders for other zones in Paradise, and at 9:17 a full-scale evacuation order went out. Many residents, including my family, never received it or were told that there was no order in effect yet. Thankfully, Paradise school leaders and staff were already mobilizing to get the children safely out of Paradise.

Meanwhile, the sky grew darker and darker until the smoke had completely blocked out the sun. This uncanny darkness figured prominently during our interviews when people spoke to us of their trauma, as did the sound of propane tanks exploding seemingly all around them. The sky rained burning bits of wood, causing the Fire to spread seemingly everywhere, all at once. One source stated that the fast winds dispersed these "wildfire embers like dandelion seeds flung into the breeze" (Gee & Anguiano, 2021). It became increasingly difficult to breathe. (Imagine movies about Pompeii and you have a pretty good idea of the situation.) By 10:00am gridlock ensued as the entire population attempted to leave through the limited arteries out of town (Epley, 2019).

Paradise is situated on a ridge between two gorgeous canyons. This geography makes it a beautiful place to live, but it also means that there are few evacuation routes (Toubman, 2019). Even with evacuation plans in place, no one had anticipated an event where the entire population of more than 26,000 Paradise residents (plus those coming through from the neighboring community of Magalia) had to evacuate all together, and so quickly (Gee & Anguiano, 2021). Unable to make headway some people abandoned their cars, trucks, and huge camper trailers, hoping they could get out faster on foot. This only increased the barriers to egress. Gas tanks began exploding.

Drivers fled as their cars caught fire. Some runners took refuge in strangers' cars. Others were picked up by the firetrucks and other emergency vehicles.

Large flames loomed on both sides of this exodus, felling trees onto some vehicles, further blocking traffic. First responders used rescue vehicles to push or bulldoze abandoned vehicles off the road to open a route, while others began hosing down school buses and other trapped cars in an effort to protect their inhabitants. Temperatures inside cars rose, with passengers later reporting burning their skin on windows and side panels. Meanwhile, some cars turned back around to seek other options, while others weaved in and out against the flow of traffic. It was a choiceless choice (e.g. Langer, 1988).[2]

Four hours after the Fire entered town, Paradise was gone. The Fire would continue burning for nearly three more weeks, eventually destroying 153,336 acres, approximately 19,000 structures, nearly 14,000 of which were family homes (Epley, 2019). Eighty-five people died, most of them in their homes. They were found in bed, in recliners, or seeking sanctuary in a shower or tub. Some were found next to the remains of beloved pets. One appeared to be clinging to a photograph. Some died just outside their houses, on porches or in carports, overtaken quickly just as they took flight. Many others died in their cars when the flames overwhelmed them. But no children died. Not a single one. Here is why.

TO CANCEL SCHOOL OR NOT?

The fact that the Paradise students were in school at all on the morning of the Fire turned out to be an arresting stroke of good luck and sound judgment. The day before, PUSD superintendent Michelle John O'Neal was attending

---

[2]This description of events was pieced together from published news reports and several personal accounts. However, everyone's experience of that morning was different. Individual accounts vary in many respects, including the timing of events and what people were told (or not told) by authorities. For example, a police officer told my family that there was no evacuation order in their zone (Zone 5) long after the evacuation order had in fact been issued. This wasn't his fault; no doubt he was given this information by a trusted source. My family left anyway. Later on they avoided the evacuation gridlock described in this book. A different police officer recommended they turn their cars around and go back to where the Fire had already crossed (Clark Road). He told them, "It will be scary, but you can probably make it." They encountered many downed powerlines and burned vehicles, but were out of town in 30 minutes. They consider themselves to be among the lucky ones. My brother offered this chillingly optimistic note near the end of his written account:

> We did not experience not knowing if the Fire would overtake our [gridlocked] parked vehicle. We did not see anyone die or believe there to be dead people in the burnt vehicles we passed. We did not get burned and only felt mild discomfort from the roadside burning.

a national superintendents' conference 600 miles away in San Diego. That evening she participated in a conference call with her two assistant superintendents, Tom Taylor and David McCready, and the Paradise School Board president, Mike Greer. These local officials informed her that the PG&E had broadcast a "watch notification" indicating that a Public Safety Power Shutoff might leave the schools without power the following day. These power shutoffs were becoming increasingly common in parts of California where wildfire risk is great. When weather reports indicated hot, dry conditions and high winds that could dislodge branches and debris onto already compromised power lines, PG&E could preemptively shut down power in impacted areas.

These watch notifications always presented a dilemma for Michelle and her team because there was no way to know in advance if the power outage was actually going to happen. More often than not, it didn't. This watch notification was merely an indication that the schools' power *might* turn off, depending on PG&E's ongoing assessment of weather conditions. In fact, a message from the Paradise Town Manager to the Town Council and staff earlier that day put the chance of shutoffs in Paradise at only 35%. The final decision was set for sometime between 4:00am and 8:00am the next morning—very inconvenient timing for busy working families who might need to make childcare arrangements. So, should they cancel school now and potentially waste a perfectly productive learning day? Or should they keep school in session on the assumption that PG&E would, as usual, keep the power on? Michelle, with the support of her team, made the call to keep school in session for now and reassess in the morning:

> They were leaning toward cancelling school until they got me on the phone. And I said, "No! We're not cancelling school!" PG&E is all talk. I said, "PG&E is all talk." And they never did. They never did shut off the electricity. And I said, "No. If they shut it off during the night, and it's gonna be shut off, that's a different matter." But I said, "Is it shut off now?" And they said, "No." And I said, "Then no."

Michelle and her team could not have known the significance of this decision. Had they canceled school, hundreds or possibly thousands of Paradise children and teens would have been home alone that morning while their parents were at work or on their way to work. It's probable that many of these students would have slept in, unaware of the danger. (Think of teenagers you know. What would they be doing at 8:00am on a weekday off from school?) They would have been trapped. No doubt their parents would have called to alert them, but powerlines and cell towers rapidly fell prey to the Fire, knocking out both cell and home phone service to much of the area. As Paradise Elementary teacher Victoria Steindorf told me,

"Tons of kids would have stayed home alone and we would have been talking about tragedies of a totally different magnitude." Michelle reflected on that day:

> In hindsight, *thank God* – I won't say "I" because we all concurred—we didn't cancel school. Because if we had cancelled school there would have been kids still at home in bed instead of on those buses and in school. And parents would have gone to work, and there would have been kids at their homes alone, and they wouldn't have been able to get out. So thank God…I don't even want to think about what could have happened. Because it didn't happen.

It did not happen. Instead, teachers, bus drivers, administrators, and other school personnel shepherded thousands of children to safety in a small, spontaneous Dunkirk of the Sierra Nevada foothills. These drivers took these children to a mustering station at the Chico Silver Dollar Fairgrounds and other places of refuge, where school personnel implemented a family reunification plan. Meanwhile, many administrators, teachers and staff stayed at the campuses, checking every cranny in every school to make sure no one was left behind. It may be the most dramatic story of *in loco parentis* ever recorded.

EVACUATING THE SCHOOLS

Paradise Intermediate (PINT) School Principal Reiner Light left his home in Paradise earlier than usual the morning of November 8 so he could drop some Halloween decorations at his storage unit. When he stepped outside he was met with an unusually dense, low smoke. It was strange, he remembered, not the usual foggy smoke he had come to expect from fire season. This smoke was more menacing, more "volcanic," like lightning should be coming out of it. He went back inside, woke his wife, and said, "Get dressed. Get dressed now. There's a Fire. I don't like the way it looks." While she got ready, he drove to an open area in town to assess the situation. He called his school secretary from his car. She explained that the Fire was two canyons away in the town of Pulga. Reiner was somewhat reassured because a previous Pulga fire had taken two weeks to travel to Paradise's adjacent Feather River Canyon. This reassurance was short-lived however, because by the time he arrived at his storage unit, flaming material was falling from the sky. He left immediately for his school. He was confident that his team was already very familiar with the District's emergency plans:

> It's one of those other things you have to do, and it's this big binder of things, and nobody really likes to go over it. And yet, because we had done that…the staff was familiar with what they were supposed to do.

One of Reiner's teachers, Tracy Parks, admitted during her interview that she had sometimes resented losing instructional time for this kind of training:

> I taught fire safety when I taught up at Pine Ridge [school] before I was up at [Paradise Intermediate] school. So I would spend about a week of history [class] time at the beginning of the year and everything was so dry. I mean, it was like *obvious*.

Her colleague Victoria Steindorf, a teacher from Paradise Elementary, interjected during my interview with Tracy: "Wasn't it required? Because I did it too."

Tracy continued:

> Well, when I taught it in sixth grade it was through the [Paradise Ridge] Fire Safe Council. And there's a whole kit and I'd spend a whole time on it...But I thought, "Ah, these kids need to know this." So I'd spend about a week talking about it. And one of the things I would tell the kids is if you're home alone, I would tell them to look at the trees. You know, we had eighty-foot Ponderosas lining these narrow streets. If those are all on fire and your parents aren't home, what are you gonna do ? And so I would tell them you need to find somebody, drive down the street, get in the car and get out. And they would say, "Well yeah, whatever Mrs. Parks." And for a lot of them that's what happened [the day of the Camp Fire]. It was crazy.

Remarkably, PINT had previously scheduled a safety plan committee meeting for the morning of the Fire. Reiner recalled:

> I walked in [to the school] you know, stuff falling out of the sky and said, "Okay, safety plan meeting!" And they looked at me like, "Really?", and I said, "Yeah, really." So we got in. I said, "All right, you! Get the box. You! Start printing all the student lists with all the contacts in case computers go down. You! Find the flashlights. You! Do that, you know. Let's get this. Let's get the student checkout list ready to go"...Burning branches are falling out of the sky, and then you're like, oh, this is serious. And I mention that because this staff was familiar with this framework, nothing had to be explained. They picked up the ball. They divided the kids up. They start checking kids out, writing down contacts.

The PINT team, like all the other Paradise schools that day, worked like a well-oiled machine built by drilling seemingly "dry and obvious" fire safety information and practicing for inconceivable and unlikely events such as this one. Reiner described some important procedures they put in place ahead of time:

> Just having the checkout sheets at the outset. Be sure you grab the emergency box. So you've got a box, and it's got all those forms. It's got the emergency plans.

Get all the keys. You know, all the stuff that your emergency plan outline is supposed to have. It's like, if your house is burning down, you're going to grab the box that has all your financial documents and your insurance and stuff.

As parents began arriving to evacuate their children, the PINT staff worked quickly to get them in cars with the right people and safely on their way. But eventually parents stopped arriving. Reiner explained:

Pretty soon everybody's heading out of town, and the number of parents coming to pick up kids dries up. And I've got like fifty kids. And so I called the bus shed and I say, "Hey, I need a bus. I got fifty kids. Nobody's coming for these guys. We gotta get out of here". They said, "We don't have any buses."

The secretary at the bus yard explained that she was trying, but she "couldn't even talk to the buses." Indeed, the repeater that drove the bus communication system was located on a hill that was burning. Reiner turned to a volunteer firefighter who was with him at the school, and they began developing a new plan: "We've got pretty good defensible space. If we have to, we can run out into the field. I think we'll be okay if we have to hunker down here."

Imagine if you will what that would be like—Fifty tweens and their protectors sheltering in a field, hoping the Fire that was currently raining embers on them would pass by or jump over. This strategy did in fact save lives in some areas of Paradise that day—notably at a Kmart parking lot (Lin II & La Ganga, 2018) and several natural bodies of water, but thankfully not at PINT. A staff member was able to get through to a spouse in law enforcement, and she was told that the sheriff was enroute to the school. When the officers arrived, they said, "Vehicle laws don't apply. We're all getting in cars, and we're getting out of here. The Fire is right over there. We're leaving in 5 minutes."

The Intermediate School staff began loading up kids into whatever vehicles remained on the property. Normally school personnel would have to obtain prior written authorization before releasing kids to leave with others or to drive them in their personal cars. PUSD bus driver Angie Van Blaricom described this scene, enacted not only at PINT, but at schools all across town: "Those teachers…just loaded kids into cars, some of them more than they should have, but they just got everybody squished in there as soon as they could, and got out of there."

Reiner and Assistant Principal Mark Abbay conducted a thorough sweep of the school, as Reiner stated, "to make sure there's nobody hiding in a bathroom. You know, some special ed kid, who's scared and hiding in a corner." Satisfied they had cleared the school, their small caravan followed the sheriff's van (also filled with children) on the comparatively unimpeded "wrong" side of the road out of town. And thus began a harrowing journey to their eventual mustering station, the Silver Dollar Fairgrounds in the neighboring city of Chico. They were the first school to arrive. Reiner and the team from PINT would later be credited taking a major leadership role in enacting the reunification processes that brought Paradise families back together again. This would lead to a brand-new role for Reiner: PUSD Camp Fire Educational Coordinator.

Reiner gives credit to his staff for executing their training while also showing extraordinary courage and initiative on November 8. He shared some advice for other administrators:

> We really built some really good teams…giving them room for initiative kind of thing. At the time of the evacuation, for example, all I was doing was going to the various groups and saying what you need? What's going on? Give me a report. But they were in charge. It's not like…I have to be the center of everything, that everything has to go through me. It's like, this is your job. I believe you know this is your responsibility. It's a big deal. But tell me what you need. And you know, just communicating and keeping the communications together and trusting your people.

Paradise Elementary

The situation was also becoming dire nearby at Paradise Elementary. Several teachers and staff stayed behind in a classroom while they waited for parents or buses to evacuate the students. Some teachers kept the children calm by playing games like Duck Duck Goose. Others made phone call after phone call, trying to locate parents. These caregivers were unaware that their school was already on fire. Fourth-grade teacher Victoria Steindorf described the scene:

> We were sitting in this classroom with the kids going, 'We're still waiting. We're still calling [parents]. No buses came to pick up our kids. So I hear pounding in the hallway and I go out there and it's the Fire Marshal and the school secretary and I'm like, "What's going on?' And he's like, "What the hell are you doing here? Why didn't you guys leave?" And I'm like, "Well we've got students. We're waiting for parents." And he's like, "You have to go! Why didn't you guys get into a bus? Why didn't you leave?" Like, no bus ever came. We're waiting for parents. And we didn't know it at that moment, but our school was already on fire at that point. And so he said, "You need to get out right now. Go to the Junior High and get on one of their buses." So we walked across the street [to PINT]. It's completely empty. They had already been evacuated. So we start walking back onto the campus and the rest of the firemen are coming though and they're like, "What are you doing? Why are you back here?" Like, there's nobody there. What do we do? So we had to just start getting in cars and, [another teacher] and I were some of the last ones.

Interested readers can search Youtube for videos made by Paradise residents on their drives out of town. What is most moving about these accounts is the adults' strategies for keeping their children calm while an inferno raged inches from their windows. They prayed, they sang, they told stories. Victoria and School Superintendent Michelle John O'Neal illuminate different aspects of these journeys. First, consider the uncertainty of making it through the Fire, given that all the predesignated "safe" places to go were also on fire. Even the PUSD's very thorough emergency plans failed to account for a situation where all of the evacuation sites simultaneously burned to the ground:

> I remember distinctly one of my principals who's been around for a long time calling me several times [during the evacuation] and saying, "Okay, we all made it to the Seventh Day Adventist Church", which was our first place to go if there was a fire. He said, "Okay, it's on fire." Then, "Okay, we made it down to Paradise Elementary." And I won't tell you all the words he used, but "It's on fire too. We're getting the hell off the Ridge." So [with planning] it's if/then, but play it out in your leadership teams because it's not going to be just one scenario. Like this one. We knew we had a plan. This is where you go. Well, crud. That place is on fire too. Here's where you go. Well crap, that place is on fire. Get off the Ridge, kind of thing.

Second, consider what you might do to keep students calm while trying to flee. Victoria recounted her experience of evacuating with another fourth-grade teacher in a car filled with four Paradise Elementary children and one dog. They immediately went into "teacher" mode, she said, turning the fiery landscape into an elementary school lesson about early California settlers:

> I crack up because…[Imitating talking to kids during a lesson] "Now. We're doing pioneers. Now, can you imagine fires happen all the time in California? So, if we were in a wagon trail, what do you think it would be like? What do you think the road would be like?" So we're talking about this and then one of the kids would start falling apart and we had another boy from her class who had wanted to be a fireman. That was his, you know, dream job. And he's like, "you know, it's gonna be okay, we're all together." And so we talked about things that we were grateful for, we talked about how grateful we weren't pioneers, we talked about what the road would have been like [in pioneer days]. [Laughs]. I can't believe that we could keep this kind of banter because I was also trying to contact parents. I had been given the school binder with all of the emergency numbers …So I was trying to contact the parents of the kids that were in the car and I just said, "I have your kid. Can I take them to my house?" Because the meeting center was…the Fairgrounds. And I'm like, "We can't just leave these kids at the Fairgrounds." And [the other teacher's] house was in Butte Creek Canyon which was also on fire so I was trying to figure out where to go and I'm just like, 'Let's just go to my house with our kids."

And it ended up I was able to contact all the parents and we met right at the bottom of the hill [in Chico].

Victoria never saw those kids again, but she has heard that one of the families settled in another city about an hour and a half away from Paradise. She does not know about the other children.

It is worth noting as part of this story that Victoria has an adult son who is nonverbal and lives with autism. While she was evacuating these Paradise Elementary students and calling their parents from the car, she was simultaneously trying to get in contact with her son's caregiver. They were also in Paradise that morning. During our interview she showed me her son's photo on her phone and explained:

> This is my autistic son who um, can often take like 45 minutes to transition. He's nonverbal and they - he wouldn't get out of the shower. So that was the other thing...I couldn't get ahold of his person and couldn't find out if they had gotten out.

I am in awe of these kinds of details. Many of the heroes evacuating other people's children from schools on November 8 did not know if their own spouses and children were safe. (Hundreds of people were still missing weeks after the Camp Fire. For example, PUSD Food Services Site Manager Linda Shields lost contact with her husband and son for *seven days*.)

In other cases, PUSD employees made arrangements for their families to leave town quickly, and instead of joining them, they went to their schools. Jacob Timm, PUSD Director of Facilities, Maintenance and Operations, called this "snapping into military." When he realized the danger, his first thought was, "I need to get these people off this Ridge in any way I can." A friend convinced Jake he could take five minutes to go to his house, less than two miles away, to rescue his dogs and grab his wife's medication: "That's because we saw the Fire, knew what the winds were doing, and figured we had the time. And so luckily we did have the time to do that before everything got totally out of control."

Meanwhile Jake coordinated with his wife to pick up their two children, his son from Paradise High School, and his daughter from her job at a local coffee shop. He called and asked them what they wanted him to grab from their house. Neither one asked for anything. He took their preprepared Go Bags, and a few other small items. Only weeks later did his son share the one thing he missed most from the house:

> When [my son] was born I had a year-and-a half old Blue Nose Pitbull, and they were thick. The minute we sat [our son] down in the car seat she just latched onto him. She was [pauses, sighs] his buddy. But we were on our way back to my sister-in-law's house [weeks after the Fire] and he said, "You know, the one thing I wish you had grabbed was Trinity." Because she was in a cremation box.

Jake is grateful for what he was able to save from home before quickly joining the two PUSD assistant superintendents in a race to clear all the schools, but he also acknowledges another feeling:

> *Jake:* I am so thankful that I got the few things that I got, but I had a lot of remorse for a long time that I got that stuff and other people didn't get anything.
> *Amber:* So a little bit of survivor's guilt?
> *Jake:* Yeah. Very much so.

Jake was able to rely on his military training during the evacuation, but most of the PUSD employees did not have this background. The humanity and selflessness of their acts leaves me speechless. They did the right thing, without a first-responder mindset or background, simply because it was the right thing. Jess Mercer shared this story:

> I remember a first-year yard duty at one of the charter schools, a very young man, I don't even remember his name, but he refused to leave and he just stood with a hose and tried to make sure the school didn't burn, to the point where somebody else had to physically push him into a car. But that level of dedication, I've never seen anything like it. Ever. And that's not even about the citizens that helped throw people into their cars, trucks, whatever it was, you know.

THE LUNCH LADY

Director of Food Services Tanya Harter arrived at her office early on November 8. One of her staff members had called in a personal day, so Tanya would be filling in for breakfast service at Achieve Charter High School in Paradise. Her office shared space with the PUSD central kitchen and a giant metal warehouse that stored all of the District's food. On normal days Food Services staff would prepare close to 2,000 meals there, so her team got to work right away. Within 45 minutes, she told me, "the world changed", and "you could just see fear on people's faces." Her husband, a Retired Battalion Chief for CAL FIRE, called her and said that everybody needed to leave. She learned that a couple of her lunch ladies had been evacuated, but no one else had received a message. She made the decision:

> I just basically called every kitchen and told my ladies–I started at the top of the hill in Magalia, and I called every school and I said, "You need to go and take care of yourselves and your family. Just put a box of peanut butter and jelly sandwiches on the counter, and if somebody's hungry, they– just go take care of your family." Because at that point every school is being evacuated. And I tell you these parts because in this place of fear and uncertainty, my lunch ladies, all they cared about was getting food to their kids. And that gave them a sense of peace that "I've left something in case there's a hungry child, and I can go, you know, do my thing."

Instead of evacuating herself, she called Assistant Superintendent David McCready and asked him how she could help. He sent her to an elementary school to assist with evacuating its children. She was there for a couple of hours, and then David sent her to another school across the street. In the meantime, she learned that some of her lunch ladies were still at the central kitchen:

> I said, "Ladies, it's time to go!" [They said] "Why? And I think they were just in shock. They really wanted to keep making lunch and not deal with what was, you know? They're not in belief that this was happening. So they left, and oh my goodness [laughing] they left all the food on the counter. In hindsight that was so horrible because these bags of chicken, by the time I got back up here in three months were just these bloated–This place smelled so bad. That was another piece to this whole puzzle that there was– the smell of rotting food is forever burned in my mind, rotting and burnt food are forever burned in my mind.

While Tanya assisted with the elementary school evacuations, she was also fielding phone calls from concerned friends and family. They were asking "Are you still there?" and imploring her to "leave leave leave." At around 10:00 in the morning, she received a desperate text from her husband:

Tanya: I guess it was about 10 o'clock in the morning, and it was *so black.* And I have this picture where there's all these ashes on my eyelashes and in my hair. And at this point, my husband had texted, and he said, "Look, I'm gonna tell you—"[crying] Sorry—this gets me.

Amber: It's okay.

Tanya: Anyway, he texted, "you better leave now, because if you don't, I'll never see you again…" I said this to him afterward, "Jeff, you used to lead entire, like battalions with a fire and arrange all these things that happen, and like how you handled me up there was the worst!" Like "I hope you didn't handle your firefighters that way." [laughing] He's like, "well, I didn't love them." [laughing] So I went inside to the principal, and I said, "Hey, how many kids do we still have here? And it was like eight kids. Eight were still there. "How many staff do you have?" it was like 15 staff. I said, "well it's time to put those kids in those people's cars and *go.*" And [the principal] is like, "I can't make that call." And I said, "well, who are we waiting for!?" So I showed [the principal] my husband's text message, and [the principal] was like "I don't know what to do." So anyway, I called [Assistant Superintendent] Tom [Taylor], but he couldn't talk because the school that they were at was on fire, and his truck was on fire, and so they—I don't know how much of their story they told you, but they had to run. So he wasn't really going to give me the answer.

Tom Taylor remains grateful for PUSD employees who took this kind of initiative:

> The staff, they were incredible...David and I are trying to manage this, organize this whole evacuation by phone, but my cell phone was dead within a pretty short time. ...But it was the people who were at the sites that were making the split-second decisions. That's what was critical in the whole situation of getting people out safely. Because you didn't have time to wait for somebody to make a call in a lot of cases.

At this point Tanya felt she had done all that she could do. Fire trucks were just pulling up to the school to evacuate the remaining 8 children and their 15 staff. She felt "really happy" about this, but the feeling was short-lived as she attempted her own evacuation:

> The road was completely blocked. And you could hear, they sounded like bombs, but they were propane tanks exploding. And I could see flames on both of my exits. And–and it was just no–no–no cars were moving. But it was dead silent. You know usually when you're in that situation people are like honking and yelling, and there's music. It was just *completely silent*.

It was also "completely black" at 10:30 in the morning. She remembered a back road, and saw that some cars were turning off to take this alternative. Not sure of the route, especially in the dark, she opted to follow their lead. But fate intervened:

> I get to the stop sign, and I look left to see if it's clear, and there's this little old lady walking down this little country road with her suitcase. And I'm thinking, Oh! It's pitch black and there's not a sidewalk. It's like this much [indicates about a foot] to the dirt. And I'm like "Hey, are you okay? Do you need something?" And she's like. "I'm just trying to get out of here." And I said, "Do you need a ride?" And she said, "I'm just trying to get out of here."

At this point in the interview Tanya shared a humorous anecdote with me. An enduring safety lesson from her parents took hold, and her first thought was to ask this little old lady if she was packing heat:

Tanya: I don't know what it was, but this like instinct from my parents clicked in, [laughing]. "Never pick up a hitch hiker! They will kill you!" So I said, "Do you have a gun?" [laughing]
Amber: [laughing] Oh my God! My dad was a police officer, so I actually get that.
Tanya: I mean seriously why would you ask that? [laughing]. And she's like, "No. Do you?"

Tanya loaded up the lady and her suitcase, but by now the cars she had been following were out of sight. She was lost:

> So I'm driving down this road and there's no flames because we're a little bit lower. But my husband is tracking me on my Find Friends on my phone, so he calls, and the phone is on speaker, you know in the car, and he just yells, "Do not go down that road or you will die!" [And I said] "Okay? Well, maybe if you could just help me get out of here that'd be great." And he's like "I don't know. I'm not familiar. I can't tell where– but the flames are right around there, just you're on the wrong road!" And the lady was so calm. and she said, "we're going to go up here, and we're going to take a left, and then we'll get on the Skway and then we'll be fine". So we did, and we finally got through that.

At the bottom of the hill Tanya encountered a group of people setting up a Red Cross shelter. She delivered her passenger into their hands, and then went to her car to retrieve some supplies. Like the other lunch ladies and their peanut butter sandwiches, Tanya felt it her responsibility to leave something behind:

> I happened to have a case of water in the back of my car, like little waters for some event that had happened the day before, and some little snacks like sunflower seeds... I brought the snacks and the water back for the Red Cross because they didn't have anything yet. So that was like the first little setup to, you know, to help out a few people who might be thirsty.

Now it was time for her to go home:

> I pulled in and my husband's all nonchalant, you know, like he didn't say much. Then he said, "Wow, you smell like a wildfire." [laughing] I said, "Oh, okay." He said, "So why don't you go take a hot tub and just kind of rinse off." And I'm like, "No, I gotta call my boss [Assistant Superintendent David McCready]. I gotta make sure he got down the hill." Then I just all of a sudden started shaking, and it was like I was *frozen*. And I couldn't stop shaking. And my husband's like, "Really, you should go get in the hot tub." And I'm like "I'm gonna call David and I'm gonna make sure he's okay." And at that point, when I talked to David, I kind of calmed down a little bit. Then I was sort of like I'm relaxed. I felt safe. And I could let go. So anyway I called David and David said they were down at the [Silver Dollar] Fairgrounds, and he said, "Hey, do you do you think you can get us some food? These kids have been in the bus since this morning."

She did indeed get them some food. Tanya and the other lunch ladies of Paradise would go on to coordinate a massive food relief program for the PUSD students. We tell this story as part of Chapter 3.

THE BUS DRIVERS

The most famous Paradise bus driver is a man named Kevin McKay. If you followed the press coverage immediately after the Fire, or have seen the 2025 Matthew McConaughey film *The Lost Bus*, you probably already know about him (e.g. Vercammen et al., 2018). He is responsible for driving 22 elementary students and two teachers out of Paradise in a five-hour ordeal that under normal circumstances would have taken about 20 minutes. When smoke began filling the bus, he took off his t-shirt, and he and the teachers tore it up and wetted it down so they could make face masks for the children. Along the way, the trio kept students from dozing off (dangerous, given the smoke), picked up a preschool teacher they found stranded along the road, and recovered from being sideswiped—hard—by a fleeing car. Kevin keeps a low profile now, partially because he went back to school to become a classroom teacher, but also because he found the nickname "Hollywood Kevin," given to him by some in Paradise after the press coverage, distasteful and unfair. He did not ask for the attention. Like everyone else in this book, he did what he could to keep children safe on November 8. His story just happened to capture the interest of some reporters, and then his particular evacuation story was repeated over and over in the press.

We did not interview Kevin for this book, but he did send an email in which he shared some thoughts and advice for other bus drivers facing extreme danger. He also provided a written endorsement (printed in the front matter of this book). We are grateful to Kevin and also his PUSD bus driver trainer, Chris Rinesmith, for reaching out on our behalf. We turn our attention now to Chris's story.

Chris Rinesmith

Chris Rinesmith had already picked up a full busload of about 30–35 students when she noticed the Fire. Almost immediately she received a radio communication requesting that she take the Ridgeview High School students to their school and drop them off. As she headed that direction, the situation changed rapidly:

> I'm getting over towards the dam going up to Old Skyway to get near the school, and just in that short time, the embers were flying in to the school site and little spot fires are starting to happen and it's just chaotic out in the parking lot and the Principal is coming out to the bus and the staff is saying, "It's not safe here! It's not safe here! You can't let any kids off!"

As Chris opened the bus doors to talk with the Principal, four children from inside the bus rushed up to the door and tried to exit. But these were not Ridgeview students. This was not their stop. These kids, and about five other non-Ridgeview children from inside the bus started talking all at once:

> "My mom's in traffic behind us. She said get off the bus now." And I'm going, "Principal! Come back! Help me out here! This is what [the students] are saying," You know, "their moms are back there." I go, "tell me, help me!" Because normally we wouldn't let them off at the wrong school site.

Here Chris struggled with an incredibly stressful decision. She is a highly trained professional who follows the rules. And the rules say, don't let the kids off at the wrong school. Don't let them get into other cars. Moreover, the person in authority who might be able to give her permission to break the rules, the Principal, was embroiled in a dozen other emergency tasks at that moment. Chris put on her "mama bear" hat and made the choice:

> You know, [the students] meant what they said. And I'm hearing what they said. And as a mom it's like, if mama bear is right there, you're gonna let the kids off. But I wasn't going to do it without them being with staff. So, the staff agreed to take those kids.

In retrospect she knows she made the correct decision, despite the cognitive dissonance it provoked:

> Letting them off when they shouldn't get off, I did do that for them. But who wouldn't? Their mom was nearby. She wants them. You know, everybody is going through a situation and getting their kids was number one. You know, if mom somehow got a communication to them, "I want you off the bus right now. I'm five cars behind, ten cars behind"...By regulation, we just *can't*. We need communication from our transportation office, but the two-way radios were down ...It's hard to be in that position when you're following all these rules and regulations and it's just - you just *can't*. You don't break the rules. But that day, we were talking on the phones while we're driving, we were doing all kinds of things we don't do out of necessity. You just did what you had to do.

Chris was then directed to take the remaining children on her bus to an evacuation point at a church. As she drove her radio communication signal began to weaken dramatically, leaving her essentially on her own. She was hoping that someone would be at the church waiting for her who could tell her next steps. But people there were just figuring things out themselves:

> So I finally got around there and I'm looking for somebody who's looking for me. Of course everybody is looking out for themselves and I'm not so sure anybody is ever gonna come to me but I'm calling on the radio, and by then I'm using my phone while I'm stopped. But eventually somebody came.

Chris wasn't sure if she was supposed to deliver all of the students to the church, or just the Ridgeview students. The staff she finally talked to told her they were accepting the Ridgeview students only. She responded, "What am I supposed to do with the other kids?" She was told to take the remaining students to the High School and then to PINT:

> Okay, back on the road. I finally get to the High School and it's chaos in there. I was able to get to the unloading area and then I've got Junior High kids saying, "My parents said to get off with my [high school] brother." And I'm not supposed to do that either. And by then it's so chaotic it's like, "Yeah, you are gonna go with your brother. Whatever your parents said for you to do, do. Listen to your brother, he's the boss."

It was scary to watch them leave, though, because the students were going in odd directions:

> They were just leaving the campus and they were going toward the bike path or something to figure it out because the parent is stuck in traffic. It's gridlock. And all you can do is let them go and wish them well, you know, and make the right best choices.

PINT was in the process of evacuating the students into the teachers' and staffs' own cars when Chris arrived, so she dropped the remaining students off. She was then asked to go to Ponderosa Elementary to assist with their evacuation. Bus driver Kevin McKay was pulling away with the last group as she arrived. Now completely alone in her bus, she was directed to go to Cedarwood Elementary to see if they needed a bus for evacuation. Let me pause here to note that the Fire was raging by now. While trying to get to Cedarwood, Chris was stuck in the S-curves, and the flames and embers are shooting across the street. She had to pace the bus's movement in between the gusts so the bus could avoid the flames and embers to the best degree. Chris kept going from school to school to school even though it must have been clear that she might not make it out of town alive.

At this point Chris had been on her bus for almost four hours, and nature called. She laughed as she told the story, but I include it in her narrative because it shows her dedication:

> It must have been 10:00 in the morning and I'd been in the bus for almost four hours and I just had to pee. [Laughs]. Nobody was in [the bus] and I was in gridlock. And so I just took the [trash] can and went over to the emergency exit. It's got a liner and I had to pop a squat and do what I had to do and wrap that thing up. [Laughing]. Double knot it! We're ditching that!

Thirty minutes later she received a message that Cedarwood Elementary had already been evacuated, and she should bring the bus back to the

PUSD bus yard. She started to do this by turning around in a Sav-Mor store parking lot, but rapidly changed her mind:

> At that point, people are dying in their cars back in town. So you know, I'm hearing, "bring the bus back to the bus yard." I'm heading towards the dam at this point and I'm knowing that that's not happening because people in front of me are turning around on the dam, making U-turns on the *dam!* One way or another, they're making U-turns in all of that chaos and gridlock. And I'm like, something's going on…And then here comes somebody I knew in a truck, a work truck, and he looks at me and I look at him, and he goes, "You don't want to go down there, people are dying in their cars." That's how I knew. And I said, "Yeah, I was feeling like I shouldn't go that way with all those people turning around. My plan is to go left on Dogtown Road and I'm gonna take Highway 32. I'm out of here."

Another empty bus followed Chris down the hill. Chris's new goal was to get down to the evacuation site at Silver Dollar Fairgrounds in Chico. But first she wanted to see if she could stop by her home, which was on the opposite side from where the Fire was traveling. She got ahold of her boss and asked, "Would you mind if I swing by the house real quick?" Once she obtained permission, she made her way there. She grabbed some chargers, snacks, a quick drink, and a few days' worth of clothes. Her husband was at the house, and he arranged to get the pets to safety. Ten minutes later she was back on the road, with the other bus following her. The other bus started having mechanical problems, so that driver had to abandon it on Highway 32 and join Chris in her bus. They both made it to the Fairgrounds safely.

When I asked Chris if she ever thought about being a hero that day, she said: "Not really. Because I was just doing what I normally do. I pick them up and I take them to school."

She also pointed to the *California Bus Drivers Training Course Instruction Manual* that she uses when training other drivers. From her perspective, her job required nothing less of her on November 8:

> When an emergency develops, every passenger looks to the driver for direction. The parents of the passengers you will be transporting expect performance from you in an emergency. It is your responsibility to know what to do…Many passengers have owed their lives to their bus drivers who were trained properly, and made the right decision at the right time. (California State Department of Education, 1990, p. 252)

The only concession Chris was willing to make is that driving school busses can be very stressful:

> They say the stress level of driving a school bus is that of somebody on the front line of a combat zone and you know, it's just pretty intense. If you're

really comfortable and experienced I think you have a better way to mitigate though and you're not going to have as high of a stress level. But I think that is probably said for like a new driver who is not as sure and their people management skills may be low.

Angie Van Blaricom

Angie Van Blaricom was a very experienced bus driver when she accepted a substitute driver position with the PUSD back in 2015. She had recently retired after a full career with the Chico Unified School District (she was Transportation Foreman when she left), and for about five years she drove fire buses, which meant taking groups of firefighters into the fray. On November 8 she was assigned to a small PUSD special education bus. During our interview, she described the start of that workday as "a normal morning." Per usual she arrived at the bus yard before 6:00am (which was prior to the first spark of the Fire at around 6:30). She picked up her Special Education aide, drove her route, welcomed her kids onto their bus, and dropped them off at Ponderosa Elementary around 7:30am. The big buses had already delivered their Ponderosa students. By now Angie could see smoke coming up from the canyon. Not long afterward she began dodging burning pine needles falling from the sky, and it became evident that "there was something going on pretty big." At around 8:00am she learned that PUSD had started to evacuate schools. She and her aide assisted other staff in loading up children onto the big bus for immediate departure. Unfortunately one of the first graders, a little boy with autism, would absolutely not get on the big bus. He would only ride Angie's bus—"his" bus.

Rather than further traumatize the child by forcing him onto the big bus, Angie's aide called the first grader's parents and offered to take him back home where his father was waiting. They didn't get very far before a fire truck stopped traffic and began hosing everyone down:

> There was a fire engine… spraying everybody down. We were at the turn signal to turn right and go up Bille Road, but we couldn't go. The Fire was coming down Bille, coming up Pence–coming up the backside. It was all around us. We must have been there about, I'm gonna say two, two and a half, maybe three hours of being sprayed down, watching people run over mailboxes as they drove down the sidewalks instead of the road. Watching people unhook trailers, leaving them in the middle of the road. People were frantic, just totally frantic.

At times like these Angie relied on her previous years of training and experience:

> There were a lot of people scared to death is all I could say. Totally scared to death of losing life…Well, you have to be calm. You have to think. You can't just

go on your gut feeling but you have to consider what's going on around you, make sure that you're as calm as possible. Yeah, it's nerve wracking. But these firefighters, they don't just go in with a gut feeling that they just gotta go and do something. They plan, they look, they know what's going on around them. And that's what you gotta do. You just can't just jump into something and do it.

She never doubted they would make it out:

Well, I didn't know for sure. But I know I watched the Fire around me. I knew we were not going to make it down the roads we were on, that we had to go up and out of that. With all of the stuff that was falling down around us, we just had to manipulate around it and stay calm. But it never did cross my mind we weren't going to make it. I just felt like we were.

Eventually the fire department declared their plan to keep the people in the trapped vehicles safe:

The fire department came down and said, "We're not going to make it here. We're going to [shelter in place at] Kmart." They were gonna move all of us to that parking lot because there were probably 150 people parked in that parking lot. So that's what we did.

It was not easy to navigate to this shelter-in-place destination:

When I made the left on Wagstaff [Road] there was a trailer right in the middle of the road. I had to navigate around it, and a telephone pole was coming down. I wasn't really sure whether we were going to make it under the telephone pole. It was leaning that far over. But we did.

Other bus drivers later recounted similar experiences with road obstacles. During our interview Angie shared an evacuation story from one of her colleagues. It echoes the tension between conscientious rule-following and Mad Max fearlessness articulated by many PUSD employees who were trying to save kids:

She was in one of our brand-new buses…There were cars parked in her way, and she didn't know how she was going to get down the road. And another driver was with her, and they could talk on the radio, and he says, "Just shove 'em out of the road with the bus!" She says, "It's a new bus!" He says, "It doesn't matter! Move the cars, get yourself out of there!" So she was very upset that she put dents in our new bus. [Laughs].

Angie, her aide, and the little boy made it safely to the Kmart parking lot. Once there, they took charge of another passenger, the 20-something, special needs relative of another bus driver:

We picked up the other driver's [relative] at the Kmart parking lot. He was just wandering around up there…We finally coaxed him into our vehicle.

He only had one shoe on...He didn't know where he was going...He was very confused, but we did bring him down [the hill], and he's safe today. So we got two [people].

This extra passenger turned out to be a blessing for other reasons. Angie's aide found some books in the parking lot donation bin and brought them back to the bus. The new adult passenger started reading to his little companion, which helped keep everyone more relaxed. Angie also focused the first-grader's attention on the car antennas swirling in the wind:

This little guy would watch...the antennas that were swirling, you know, telling you that the wind was blowing, and I would tell him to watch that. You know, "If there's any air I want to know." And he'd watch for that. "Air Angie! Air! Air! It's coming!" So we entertained him in that way. He was just a sweetheart of a child.

When it was safe to do so, a firefighter gathered water bottles from one of the stores bordering the parking lot. Angie's first grader was eager for a drink, as he hadn't had water in hours. Other refugees had motorhomes and trailers, and they were "wonderful" about sharing their stores of food. The group spent about four hours at Kmart before they were released to evacuate down the hill to Chico. The Fire encircled their position for most of this time. Angie estimated that it was about 7:00 or 8:00 at night when they finally left. During all these hours Angie and her aide had continuously tried calling the first grader's father, but they could not reach him. His mother, she said, "had no idea where we were." It turned out that the little special education bus was the last bus to leave Paradise that day. Angie showed me a photograph of the caravan of vehicles leaving Kmart that night:

At that point, Safeway was ablaze. All the stores along the side were. Notice the picture...of us escaping. I'm the little bus with the caution lights blinking so people would follow me because it was dark. It was so dark up there. And we would just be navigating down. We got almost to Orville, turned, and came back up to Chico and to the church where everybody was...I mean, when we drove down there at the church, of course everybody was so overwhelmingly delighted because the repeaters went down, so we had no contact with the radios or anything like that. We couldn't contact anybody. They had had no transmission from us, and they thought we were gone because we were on that road that was being engulfed.

The first-grader's mother was waiting at the church, and you can imagine the reunion. Angie has since heard that their family has relocated to another city in California.

When I asked Angie if she thought the little boy was aware of his peril on November 8, she responded:

No. I don't think so at all. I don't think he was aware. He was just entertained by us. And he would make stories up...He had a vivid imagination...And he was our clown on our bus. He was just a sweet, sweet kid.

However, she noted that students had many different responses to the trauma:

I think some of them were very battered by what happened that day. The kids, most of them that I had, worked out all right....I got two of the kids that I had on my route [on November 8] now that are older. They're resilient. I mean, they do adapt. Kids do adapt. I don't know how deep it goes into some of them. I have one little girl... that just stopped talking. She's now talking, saying hi and stuff. They've worked with her and stuff. So it hit some of them really hard, and then other ones it's like it never happened.

When I mentioned to Angie that I thought her actions were heroic, she demurred: "We did our thing. It wasn't that we were heroes or anything and we didn't want everybody to be 'Wow! Wow!' We did what we needed to do because we love these kids."

Checking the Schools

Assistant Superintendent of the PUSD Tom Taylor woke up on November 8, and seeing the Fire from his window, immediately understood the peril; this situation was "dangerous" and "life-threatening." He engaged in a quick discussion with his wife. Once ensured of his family's safety, he had one thing on his mind: "I have to get to the schools." He began with Ponderosa Elementary, assisting the teachers and staff who were loading children onto Kevin McKay's evacuation bus:

Tom: We had an incredible, I mean, our employees, the staff—Everybody talks about heroes in situations. Honestly, the staff did just incredible...The majority of the people did just the right things, which was doing what most people would do, you know, in that horrible situation.

Once the Ponderosa bus was safely on its way, Tom rechecked the whole campus. From there he made the 0.8-mile trip to the PUSD District Office, where he met up with David McCready, Assistant Superintendent of Business Services. At that point driving had become impossible, so they set off together on a surreal expedition in darkness and on foot to check other schools. Early on in the trek they were able to take and receive calls, and they were reassured to hear that Principal Larry Johnson had declared Paradise High School to be clear of students and staff:

Tom: I remember Larry Johnson, who is a combat veteran. I found out he said the [High] school was evacuated. And knowing him and his background, and how he reacts in tough situations, I was very confident.

But cell towers and power lines were coming down all over town, and almost immediately they lost communication with the other schools. They had to visit each one in person:

Tom: I mean driving really wasn't an option. We felt we had to check the schools and make sure all the schools were evacuated...We lost communication. So walking was really our only choice to get to the schools to see.
David: Because you couldn't—The traffic wasn't moving. In a perfect world, if we could pick now, we would have had motorcycles here. Motorcycles would have been absolutely great.

The evacuation congestion was so bad that they actually caught up to the Ponderosa Elementary bus, the one that had been first to evacuate, the one they thought was safe. Readers will appreciate the gravity of the decision Tom Taylor had to make in that moment:

Tom: We actually caught up with the bus right here and we had kids on it. In my mind I was like, "Do I take all these kids and get them off the bus right now and have them walk to the schools with me, or do we leave them on the bus?" We actually got on the bus, and I felt like taking them off the bus, but it was going to be *just too devastating* to them. I think they felt like they had security. Right or wrong, that's the decision that was made.

It turned out to be the right decision. But as Tom and David continued their terrible journey, it wasn't always clear which way they needed go to get to each school. So much was burning. Having a partner was incredibly important to keeping them calm and purposeful.

Tom: There were some points where had we gone certain directions, I think we would have been okay? [looks at David] But it was interesting that I was never—The day of the Fire I was never fearful because I was next to [David] if that makes sense. Had I walked out by myself, I think I would have felt differently. But I never—There's something about being in a team, all of a sudden, that I wasn't fearful. We *were* getting out of there.

David: Yeah.

Tom: …It was a feeling of—having somebody else that you're *with* makes such a difference. And I think that expands to the whole community…You know when you have somebody else there going through something with you, it's going to be better. No matter how bad it is, having somebody with you, it's going to be better.

Tom and David were also eager to connect with Jacob Timm, PUSD Director of Facilities, Maintenance and Operations. They knew he was also checking schools. At some point they left a note for Jake on a small building owned by the District, but that building caught fire before he was able to retrieve it. Tom and David still tease Jake about this: "We left you a note on the door, and we're waiting [for your response]!" They eventually caught up with him at the PUSD Transportation Office, home base for the heroic bus drivers who helped rescue a generation of Paradise children. The three men discovered, to their surprise, that they were not alone:

Tom: We had an employee at the Transportation [Office] and we get there and we're like, "What are you doing—Jaime, you gotta go! What are you–" And she goes, "I'm answering phones." And she has her two kids with her. And she says, "I gotta—We gotta make sure–" And she was like everybody else, "We gotta be sure kids get to safety." And David looks at her and says, "*You need to leave.* You gotta get your kids and get outta here." And about that time the power went out. And she goes, "I guess I'm leaving."[3]

The team then moved next door to check that Paradise Elementary had been fully evacuated.

It is difficult for Tom and David to estimate how long this trek lasted, as time is notoriously hard to pin down in crisis situations. But once they were satisfied that every school was empty, they sought their own egress out of town. There had been times, they admitted, when they weren't sure which route to take. At one point during the interview when Tom was describing where the Fire was relative to their position ("It was *right there*"), he looked over at David inquisitively and said, "I *think* we would have made it?" Thankfully they found someone to help them escape. Here, at many other times during our interview, the men shared a humorous anecdote:

---

[3] Jaime initially agreed to be interviewed for this book, but ultimately decided it would be too painful to recount those memories. This speaks to the long-term mental health implications of the fire. As my brother told me, "For us, the day of the Fire may have been one of the easier ones."

David: Tom found a wonderful person that let us jump in the back of their truck. So as we're heading out of town, …there's flames on both sides. It's not like the heat was very close, but you could feel it. And we're looking at each other. It's dark. And this guy [the truck driver] was *moving*, and you know, I wear a lot of gel in my hair. [smiling]

Tom: [laughing]

David: So the funny part was, in this very serious moment when people's houses are on fire on both sides of us, and we were leaving, Tom looks over at me and –'cause we were *flying*. We were probably going—[to Tom] How fast *were* we going?

Tom: 100, 85 miles per hour. [laughing]

David: [laughing] It was *fast*. I don't know how fast it was, but this guy *was not dying on that hill*, and Tom looks over at me in this very serious moment and he goes, "David! I think your hair product is failing!" [all laughing]

David: It's like one of those funny things. It was so funny at the time. So when we get to the bottom of the hill, we got out of the truck. And I said [to the truck driver], "Thank you, man. You saved us. I mean, you got us out of there." And I said, "You've got some real driving skills. You want to drive a school bus?" And the guy said, [imitating a gruff voice], "Nah. I'm not that good with kids."
[all laughing]

Tom and David remain reticent to share certain details of their November 8 story, as they are eager to avoid attention or praise for what are undeniably heroic acts. (I heard about these acts from others). Tom worries that in telling the story of one individual, others equally important or more important may be ignored. This is indeed the case in a book such as this one, where every story of heroism must stand for hundreds more. Tom was also gracious in his estimation of those who were not able to respond with great daring:

Tom: You know, it isn't one person that day. Everybody played a part. I want to be careful saying that, because some people can't act in a situation, and I can't—that's okay. I mean it was scary, and some people's reactions were a little bit different. But *so many* people, the majority by far, reacted in such an incredible way that there isn't *one story*. I mean, everybody has a similar story about getting people out, staying with their classroom, calling parents, being sure that the kids are picked up. And it's not just that it's putting kids in your car and getting down the hill the best that you can. It's really that there's *so many*. There's not one story. I think to try to put a single name to a story, when everybody was doing so much, would discredit some people and I don't want to.

PERSONAL LOSSES

PINT School Principal Reiner Light would later learn that his home burned to the ground on November 8. His wife, Tina, was caught in the evacuation gridlock, but made it safely out of town after choosing to drive down the "wrong" side of the road. Reiner believes this decision saved her life. His teacher Tracy Parks lost her home, her father's home, and her in-laws' home that day. Jacob Timm, PUSD Director of Facilities, Maintenance and Operations, lost his home. Bus driver/driver trainer Chris Rinesmith's family home was spared, but she was displaced for weeks. The father of her children lost his home, and with that, many of their children's possessions. One of her sons lost his home, and he was mildly burned trying to save it. He was renting, and his possessions were uninsured. Chris also lost three underinsured rental properties that were part of her retirement plan. Her daughter's dog, Chopper, was gravely burned, but he was saved by a cutting-edge Tilapia fish skin grafting treatment at the University of California, Davis. Bus driver Angie Van Blaricom lost her car and her computer. Superintendent Michell John O'Neal's home survived, but her family was displaced for 6 months. Assistant Superintendent Tom Taylor's home was also spared, but his family was displaced for weeks. He also lost his truck. Assistant Superintendent David McCready, Paradise Elementary teacher Victoria Steindorf, and Director of Food Services Tanya Harter lived in undamaged communities outside the burn scar. But nobody lost children. We end this chapter as we began it, with a quote from Tom Taylor:

> Every kid made it, every staff member made it, which is pretty much a miracle. I mean, the staff, they were incredible, throwing kids in their cars…it was the people who were at the sites that were making the split-second decisions…It goes back to what everybody did at their own site that day, and being sure they were taking care of kids, which is what an educator's job is.

REFERENCES

California State Department of Education. (1990). *California bus drivers training course instructor's manual.* California State Department of Education.
Gee, A., & Anguiano, D. (2021). *Fire in Paradise: An American tragedy.* WW Norton & Co.
Johnson, L. (2021). *Paradise: One town's struggle to survive an American wildfire.* Crown.
Langer, L. (1998). The dilemma of choice in the deathcamps. In A. Rosenberg, & G. E. Myers (Eds.), *Echoes from the Holocaust: Philosophical reflections on a dark time* (pp. 118–127). Temple University Press.

Lin II, R.-G., & La Ganga, M. L. (2018, December 2). They thought they'd die trapped in a parking lot. How 150 survivors of California's deadliest fire made it out alive. *Los Angeles Times.* https://www.latimes.com/local/lanow/la-me-ln-paradise-survivors-20181202-htmlstory.html

Vercammen, P., McLaughlin, E. C., & Simon, D. (2018, November 19). 'Bus driver from heaven' rescued children from California wildfire. *CNN.* https://www.cnn.com/2018/11/18/us/wildfire-school-bus-rescue/index.html

CHAPTER 3

REUNITING PARENTS AND CHILDREN

Nobody has a plan for when your whole town burns down…Nevertheless, they adapted it and made it happen. And I am so proud of those people for doing that, because you know, the parents were just like, "Thank you. Thank you for doing it right. Thank you for looking after our kids."

—Reiner Light, Camp Fire Educational Coordinator

Having safely evacuated the children of Paradise, it was time to reunite them with their parents. Principal Reiner Light's team from Paradise Intermediate (PINT) was the first to arrive at the Silver Dollar Fairgrounds in Chico. This refuge was not part of the original school evacuation plan, but every previously-identified option was burning. The Fairgrounds, approximately 20 miles from Paradise, seemed a good choice for a large-scale evacuation such as this one. Prior to leaving PINT, Reiner's team placed notes on school doors (on the chance the school made it through) and sent out an all-call message to parents informing them of their destination. Unfortunately, the evacuees were turned away when they arrived at the Fairgrounds. The California Department of Forestry and Fire Protection (CAL FIRE) had already claimed the space, and would be arriving that afternoon. Reiner described the scene:

> When I got there everybody's out in the parking lot, and I said, "Can we get into a building?" They said, "Oh, no, we can't." So I went in to talk to the guy, and I said, "Hey, we need space. It's cold out here. I've got these kids."

When the Fairgrounds representative reiterated his position, Reiner pushed: "I said, 'You see that smoke? That's my town. It's on fire. Those people up there think their kids are here at the Fairgrounds...This is where we're going to be.'"

The Fairgrounds agreed to open up one wing for the Paradise students, and Reiner's team began implementing a system to reunite families. Almost immediately they set up a table and had a check-out system in place. It was a marvel of efficiency that Reiner credits to preparation, practice, and "trusting your people." The teachers and staff obviously could not access the District's Aries Student Information system because all the servers were down in Paradise. Fortunately, they knew what to grab on their way out of the school. Reiner offered some recommendations:

> Be sure you grab the emergency box. So you've got a box, and it's got all those forms. It's got the emergency plans. Get all the keys. It's got all the stuff that your emergency plan outline is supposed to have. You gotta make sure. It's like if your house is burning down, you're going to grab the box that has all your financial documents and your insurance and stuff.

Reiner described some of these important documents:

> In our safety plan we have the checkout sheets, and the student's name, it has contact numbers, it has the, you know, who picked them up, what they're driving, the license number, etc. And so, you know, we just had bunches of copies of those for our kids. And so that's what the teachers had on clipboards.

Current Paradise Unified School District (PUSD) Superintendent Tom Taylor (Assistant Superintendent at the time of the Fire) expressed his admiration for the PINT administrators, teachers, and staff in the following quote from his interview:

> You know we talk about a plan of reuniting kids with their parents in the case of a disaster. And we had the plan, and it was critical. And I have to credit Reiner Light and his staff...His staff was one of the first groups to make it to the Fairgrounds, and they actually set up the whole system for reuniting families. I mean we had a general plan, but they really put it into play. And you can imagine, you have hundreds of parents coming, just panicked, not knowing if their child is there or not there. And that staff did an incredible job...They were just there making sure everybody got connected to the right place. I think by that night we had connected people, and that was pretty incredible... It's a piece nobody thinks about, but it was a really important piece, because I mean, think of a child. You could have been a six year-old, seven year-old kid that was thrown in a car, you know, with your teacher, and you're running, racing down the hill to avoid the Fire, and you don't know where your parents are. Your parents don't know where you are. And even our older kids—they

understood the magnitude of it. But that's probably a part that nobody really talks about. And it was really a critical part in that whole day.

FEEDING THE STUDENTS

Meanwhile, small snacks and bottled water started showing up at the Fairgrounds, probably provided by local churches or service organizations. Everyone was very grateful for this, because they had already spent hours without food or water. Recall that Assistant Superintendent David McCready had asked PUSD Director of Food Services, Tanya Harter, to try to get some food to the Fairgrounds. This was about noon. Tanya had just escaped through the Fire and made it home, smelling like wildfire, and with ashes on her eyelashes. She went right back into the fray. David and PUSD Superintendent Tom Taylor recalled.

> *Tom:* So Tanya—Ah, Tanya. Tanya was getting food for people. I mean this is a story here. Tanya was getting food trucked—
> *David:* The. Day. Of. The. Fire.
> *Tom:* Yeah.
> *David:* She worked with Chico Unified and got food for all the kids.
> *Tom:* I don't even know where she got food. But she was getting food from everywhere, it seemed like.
> *David:* But that *day*, within—12:30, we're showing up at the Fairgrounds and she's already got food for the kids that were down there.

What Tanya had done was leverage her relationship with one of her prior employers, the Chico Unified School District. She had worked in their Food Services department for 11 years before to moving to PUSD. She called her previous boss, Vince, and asked if she could "come grab some food" because there were about 300 hungry kids at the Fairgrounds. Vince was eager to help, offering sandwiches, milk, fruit, and fresh baked chocolate chip cookies. As luck would have it, the Fairgrounds were located just behind Chico Unified. They grabbed a truck and loaded everything up. Tanya described the scene. The trauma was very fresh:

> We went over to the Fairgrounds, and it was very chaotic because people were just starting to roll in. And the first thing I did was go to the buses because I knew that's where the kids were. Well, they were all just filing out to let the kids go to the bathroom. And the bus drivers [long pause, emotional] they were...one of them, when I came up because I had my badge on and they knew who I was– and one of them came up and gave me a big hug, and she says, "I quit. I don't want to do this job anymore." Like, you know. What do you say?

After a few moments with the bus driver, Tanya went in search of David McCready, who she described as looking uncharacteristically disheveled after his adventures checking the schools with Tom Taylor. They shared a brief moment of levity. "You're not going to believe what we did!," David said, "and I just listened, because you could tell he just had to let some of that out."

Before Tanya could begin serving food, it was time to leave the Fairgrounds. CAL FIRE would be arriving soon, and they were delivering convict crews to the site. A PUSD employee called a local Church of Jesus Christ of Latter-day Saints (LDS), and their congregation agreed to welcome everyone to their campus. PUSD loaded the students back onto the buses and the drivers headed to the church. Any new buses that arrived at the Fairgrounds were diverted to the new location. Tanya's truck carrying the food followed the buses. It took about an hour to traverse the short distance to the church. As soon as they arrived volunteers unloaded the boxes of food while teachers and staff helped the children file through a makeshift lunch line. For many, it was their first nourishment that day. But it wouldn't be the last. The LDS church was incredibly well-prepared to help. David McCready explained:

> It was amazing how fast they had food for everyone. It was a well-oiled machine. It was impressive. I mean even our eye doctor [an LDS member], he was doing security on the outside. And I was like, "What are you doing?" And he was like, "Oh, I got off work so I'm over here. I'm going to run security for the next six hours." And I was like, "What?!" [And he said] "Oh yeah. I don't have to be back at work until tomorrow." It was impressive all the people that came together to help.

While church staff and volunteers attended to the children and their PUSD caregivers, the PUSD administrators, teachers and staff mobilized. First on the agenda: Survey everyone and create a master list with every student's name and their school. This way, they could keep track of children they released, and provide up-to-date information to any parent who called the church looking for their child: We could say, "Yes, they were picked up by such and such or so and so." Assistant Superintendent David McCready estimates that the last child was reunited with family at around 12:30am. Michelle thinks it was closer to 1:00am. This child's grandparent drove 6 hours to get to Paradise because no one could locate his parents. Fortunately, someone was able to connect with his parents within a day or two after the Fire.

The organizational system was remarkably effective. Only two children went missing, and only temporarily. Reiner Light told me about one of these:

> There's one parent at the Fairgrounds who was looking for a special ed kid, and they weren't there. And you know they checked in a couple of times, and

then when we went to the LDS church everybody is telling me you know, all the buses are accounted for, and everything else like that. And this one kid was missing. And the parents are starting to get a little weirded out. And I go out in the parking lot, and there's this little bus parked over on the side, and I saw people in it and I go, "What are you guys doing?" [And the caregiver said,] "Oh, we're waiting for somebody to pick up this kid." They had not come to the front of the school. They're just sitting there, and this kid is in there. Hallelujah. Out on the radio I said, "Send the parents over. We got their kid." Yeah, amidst the chaos, there were little miracles like that.

Tom Taylor also shared a story about another missing PUSD student who had not been at the Fairgrounds or the LDS church. He still finds the memory distressing:

Tom: The first couple of nights [after the Fire]...I'd watch TV and [pause] every night I was watching for that kid's name on there. And that was just—That was one of the hardest things, I think, for me, is—I mean it would have been hard for everybody, but it did go through my mind. We had a dad that couldn't find their kid, which not many people know about. I honestly don't remember how many days it took. It seemed like three days. It might have been one day. But *we could not find one kid.* And they ended up being in [another city].
Amber: With who?
Tom: [sigh] I don't really remember. I think I have a note on it, but it was with her mom or a friend, or something like that. But the dad was saying, "what am I—" I mean, how do you tell a parent, you know? But that was kind of tough, too, watching the news. You know, I mean we know we lost a lot of people. It was just scary thinking that—when it's kids it's just so hard.

And so ends the first full day of the PUSD triumph over the 2018 Camp Fire. Now that the kids were safe, it was time to save the District itself. As Assistant Superintendent David McCready told me, "We never stopped fighting from that night."

CHAPTER 4

KEEPING THE STUDENTS TOGETHER

I give a lot of credit to [Superintendent] Michelle...She said, "You know what? We can do this." She and Tom Taylor said, "We can do this." And right there the switch flipped, and it was, "Okay, what do we need to do to ensure that we can get these kids back in school?" It gave everybody a sense of purpose instead of feeling lost again.

—Jacob Timm, PUSD Director of Facilities, Maintenance, and Operations

When the Fire subsided, the Paradise Unified School District (PUSD) community faced another existential threat: Statute 300.101 of the United States Individuals with Disabilities Education Act. This important federal law requires that all students have access to a Free and Appropriate Public Education (FAPE). Unfortunately, PUSD could no longer provide FAPE, because so many of their campuses had been destroyed, damaged, or were otherwise inaccessible for the foreseeable future. Moreover, approximately 70% of their employees and nearly all of their students had lost their homes and were scattered across the state and the country. Given these circumstances, it seemed inevitable that Butte County would dissolve the District, and the PUSD students would disperse to get their FAPE elsewhere. But this is not what the Paradise parents or students wanted. Having lost nearly everything else that was stable in their lives, the students wanted to stay connected to their friends and their teachers. Their parents implored PUSD leadership to find a way to make this happen. This chapter explains how the people of the PUSD exercised "sheer determination and guts" to do just that.

FIRST TRIP BACK TO PARADISE

The day after the Fire, PUSD Superintendent Michelle John O'Neal, Assistant Superintendent Tom Taylor, Director of Facilities, Maintenance, and Operations Jake Timm, and Director of Food Services Tanya Harter acquired permission to enter the barricaded town of Paradise. No official escorts were available, so Tanya's husband Jeff (a Retired Battalion Chief for California Department of Forestry and Fire Protection) was granted permission to serve in this role. The group wanted to survey the extent of the damage to the schools and salvage any items that would be immediately useful. Of particular interest were the PUSD computer servers and any food remaining in the central kitchen and its freezers; there were plenty of hungry, displaced students who could benefit from that stash. The team was somewhat optimistic about the food, given the chilly weather that day. Tanya remembers, "It was very cold. Even though the world was on fire... It was freezing."

Having Jeff as an escort was necessary because Paradise was a very dangerous place. Hazards abounded—downed powerlines, spot fires, toxicity, trees ready to fall any second, just obstacles everywhere. The team thought they were prepared, but Jeff reminded them that this was not all. No one yet knew the number of victims, and search and recovery had only just begun. It was possible that they would encounter a grisly scene. Tanya recalled: "Jeff, my husband, was very clear. He said I should not look around too much because 'I'm not sure what you'll find.' And so I kind of kept my blinders on."

Some people were consumed by the Fire while they were trying to escape in their vehicles, so Jeff's caution was warranted. Thankfully the PUSD team did not see death on this trip.

Tanya's mood elevated when they pulled into the PUSD central kitchen. Half of the building was gone, but the giant freezer seemed to be intact. The team cut the lock off and investigated:

> I slid the thing open, and all this smoke came out. It was burning. *It was still burning.* So that was kind of devastating, because...probably eighty thousand dollars worth of food was in that freezer. But my little [freezers] were fine, and it turns out that was a good thing, because all the food in that [giant] freezer was like whole chickens and hamburger patties and things you can't just open up and give to people. My two little freezers had things like muffins that were wrapped, and little breakfast things and snacky things. So that was perfect. We made a conveyor line of people, and we just started loading everything up, and we drove everything back down to Chico Unified [School District]...We just shoved it all in there until we could figure out how we were going to dispense it to the community at that point. We had the help of City of Chico's Waste Management (new dump truck) to help haul food down to Chico. They were so kind to help us out.

As the team made their way from school to school for the first time, the magnitude of the devastation was obvious. I think many school leaders would be tempted to throw in the towel, but this group chose to be motivated by what remained. Jake Timm explained:

> I give a lot of credit to Michelle…One of our first stops was at Paradise Elementary [which had burned to the ground]. But then we saw that the Junior High had made it. And she said, "Okay, it's bad but so far it's not too bad." And then we saw Paradise High school [was still standing] and she said, "You know what? We can do this." She and Tom Taylor said, "We can do this." And right there the switch flipped, and it was, "Okay, what do we need to do to ensure that we can get these kids back in school?" It gave everybody a sense of purpose instead of feeling lost again.

TRIAGE

That same day, Michelle, Tom, and Assistant Superintendent of Business Services David McCready convened at the home of the PUSD attorney and began to triage. One day earlier on November 8, their goal had been to get everyone out of their schools and into places of safety. Today their goal was to bring them back. Their first step was to contact all of the principals and invite them to a planning meeting and breakfast to take place on November 12 at the home of Michelle's cousin. (This family took in Michelle's family after the Fire.) Consistent with the "people first" stance PUSD would embrace going forward, this breakfast provided an important time for reconnection and fellowship. Michelle explained during our interview that an essential goal for all PUSD meetings after the Fire was to let everyone know "they're loved, cared for, and together."

This mutual support was essential for the PUSD's sustained objective of getting the Paradise students back to school. At the November 12 breakfast meeting the three superintendents asked each of the principals to locate their own teachers and staff (not an easy proposition, since communication that first week was essentially "non-existent"), and to bring each of these school teams together for their own breakfast meetings. These could take place in homes, restaurants, or any available space. A major priority was letting those teachers know they would be supported and cared for as they navigated their own personal losses and displacement. These teachers were also key players in the next steps: Finding the children of Paradise and bringing them together with their classes. Many PUSD employees told me during their interviews that these early gatherings were the beginning of the most difficult and meaningful challenge of their careers. Tom explained during his interview:

> I mean there were *so many* decisions to be made. I mean, how do you even— How do you put, what, 2000 kids, in places when your schools are gone and you can't come back to your town?

LEGAL CHALLENGES

Tom Taylor's question was a very good one. How *do* you do that? The answer from the Butte County Superintendent made sense at face value: Since the PUSD doesn't have schools, it can't provide the FAPE that Federal law requires. Therefore, displaced families should enroll their children in schools in other districts. However, whenever Michelle or any of her PUSD employees spoke to displaced families, they implored them to keep their children with their friends and their teachers. They kept telling her "It's the *only* piece of stability they have. It's the *only* thing they have." Their teachers, most of whom were also displaced and dealing with their own loss and trauma, concurred. Michelle remembers:

> When we said to the teachers, "What do you need from us? How can we help you?", they all said, "We need our kids. We need our kids together." I said, "Okay, that's what I'm going to try and do then."

Michelle understood FAPE very well, and valued it, but she thought the County Superintendent's decision was premature. The Fire had temporarily closed the whole County through Thanksgiving, so nobody was in school yet anyway. She argued:

> "Sending the kids away when they're not even in school yet–They don't even go back until December! Let me see what I can do." Of course we were working around the clock from the day of the Fire until then. [I said], "Let me see what I can do, so I can do what the parents and the kids and the teachers want. They all want to be together."

But it was a fierce battle, sometimes involving "harsh words" with the County. Michelle remembered:

> They kept reminding me—"The law is we have to provide a place for education, and you don't have a place." And I'm saying, "Okay, I *will* have a place. Stop telling them to go sign up [in schools] where they are total strangers."

A few parents heard the message from Butte County first, so they proceeded to enroll their students in outside schools. This was not successful:

> Parents did do that, and then they came right back. The parents were crying, their kids were crying, and their kids were hiding. So may sad stories. Kids were hiding in corners of other places because parents went out and signed them up for different schools and districts. We pretty much had it together [after Thanksgiving] but sometimes communication was so bad that the parents didn't know. So there was some trauma caused. And I understand that law. I understand "free and appropriate public education", and that's true.

But the emotional needs of the kids needed to take precedence at this time. And they needed to be with their teachers and friends who loved them.

As PUSD Director of Facilities, Maintenance and Operations, Jacob Timm further explained, the Paradise children were now too different from their peers; they weren't understood in their new schools, and they couldn't connect with the other kids. They were also living in tents and trailers and motels. They needed "that sense of normal" that only their own teachers and friends could provide: "These [outside] kids can't assimilate with what happened to our kids. I mean, we've had people move out of state that have come back [to PUSD] because they're just like, 'people don't understand it.'"

Moreover, the students needed to see for themselves that their friends were alive and well. Leaving the District meant they didn't see their peers, and the media accounts of missing and dead people were scaring them: "It was huge for them…Just knowing their friends were safe. Nobody had any contact. Once the cell service went down up here, nobody had any idea what was going on."

FINDING NEW LOCATIONS FOR THE PUSD SCHOOLS

Within a couple of days after the Fire Michelle appointed Paradise Intermediate (PINT) School Principal Reiner Light to a newly created role of Camp Fire Educational Coordinator. One major responsibility for this new position would be helping to find places to put schools. Reiner explained:

> Tom and Michelle and David established right up front that, "No, we're keeping this District alive." And so that became the mission. Because of that, because of their determination, this is Paradise Unified. They said, "We're keeping it together." Then that was it.

On November 14 Butte County held a meeting in Chico to give status updates and brainstorm education options for the PUSD students. The search for real estate had already begun; Reiner's notes for this begin on November 12. Reiner, Michelle, and other senior members of the PUSD administrative team had begun contacting school districts, churches and businesses that might be suitable for temporarily housing schools. They had insurance funds to cover the cost of renting these spaces, so that would actually benefit these potential landlords. The neighboring Districts of Chico Unified, Oroville City Elementary School District, Oroville Union High School District, and Durham Unified were extraordinarily supportive. For example, Oroville City Elementary School District moved their own students out of Bird Street Elementary and relocated them so that PUSD could then move Paradise Elementary in. PUSD then added portables to increase the school's capacity. Oroville Union High School District temporarily housed PUSD senior leadership at their Adult Education Career and Technical Center in Chico. Durham USD gave up a section of Durham Elementary to house Paradise's Ponderosa Elementary, and again PUSD added portables. Chico Unified offered their central kitchen, a food truck, two food delivery vans, provided office space for PUSD food service, and generally buttressed all of PUSD's recovery efforts. Metaphorically speaking, Chico Unified was the supportive local family that watched out for PUSD during its darkest hour. During their interview, David and Tom made a special request that I convey their gratitude to all three districts in this book. As David put it, "You don't just move a school district from one town to another without a lot of help." Reiner recalled how the neighboring districts anticipated their needs:

> This is what's amazing about people here...I would call Durham, and say, "Hey. this is the landline from Paradise Unified. I'm just calling the superintendent to find out what kind of classroom space they have." They had already inventoried their schools! These people already had this stuff at their fingertips! It wasn't like, "Let me look, and I'll get right back to you."

But PUSD needed more space than these helpful districts could provide. Michelle, Tom, David, Reiner, and their team cast a wide net, but options were limited. The disaster didn't just impact the schools—it impacted the whole county. This meant that PUSD was competing for space with all of the agencies that had just moved in to help with recovery. These organizations moved quickly to secure real estate, as this was something they did routinely in cities all over the country. David and Tom explained:

David: We were competing with all the agencies like FEMA and all the insurance companies that came in. They would rent the Sears building, you know, and all those places in the [Chico] mall

Tom: They were good at it.

David: They got in there, so we were competing for some of those buildings so that we could put schools in them. So that made it very challenging.

Tom: Yeah. So we would contact them and they would say, "I'm sorry. such and such is [already rented by] you know, Red Cross, whatever agency." These are all good agencies wanting to help out, but *that's what they do*. They come in, they see a disaster like this, and they just start renting everything.

During this process PUSD leadership visited many potential spaces that turned out to be unsuitable for various reasons, but out of desperation they considered them. Michelle recalled:

Some of the school settings just weren't "it." It just wasn't going to work out. It was either, you know, a classroom here and a classroom there where kids were going to be broken up, or staff is going to be broken up, or the kids were going to have to be absorbed into the school, which we really didn't want. We wanted to keep each school together…There were just so many weird things. Like there was an empty racquetball club that we actually kind of considered because it had these racquetball courts that could act like classrooms, but they were really echo chambers and it smelled like old chlorine, and the building was really musty, and it was like, ugh. But we were getting desperate. We were like, "Well, this is in the running."

Two of the commercial spaces the team visited in Chico rose to the top: The former Facebook building at the airport, and a former Orchard Supply Hardware (OSH) store. This book offers a portrait of the OSH school in Chapter Five. The Facebook building was attractive for a variety of reasons. Reiner told me:

The Facebook building out there at the airport–obviously everybody wanted it, because it had already had built in I.T. It was carpeted. It would be easy to divide up into classrooms. It just looked like a nice building, you know. They had a large warehouse area where you could do PE or your crafts or whatever.

This space would end up working well as the second temporary home of Paradise, but like all the successful sites, some modifications needed to be made first. Reiner explained:

We used some money to buy a lot of the soundproof dividers, you know, little office divider things to make classrooms, but it worked out pretty good for them. Then we got some donated weightlifting equipment, and they made a makeshift gym down in the warehouse, and kids would play football in the grassy field behind it. They also got some basketball hoops and put them out back.

By November 26—only 18 days after the Fire—PUSD had established where many of their schools would meet, with a goal of opening most sites to students on December 3. For example, Paradise Elementary would move into the vacated Bird Street school in Oroville USD; Ponderosa Elementary would take over part of Durham Elementary in Durham USD; Ridgeview High would move into the Chico Boys and Girls Club. Paradise High School and PINT would temporarily utilize two adjacent storefronts in the Chico Mall for drop-in independent learning support. This was much like what would eventually happen across the country during Covid-19. As Tom explained, "It was more check-in for students. They would come in and get their Chromebooks. There would be like a, 'come in and see your teacher'—It was more of a connection-type thing."

The mall turned out to be surreal experience for some PUSD teachers and staff. Dena Kapsalis, PUSD Director of Student Services described some unnerving aspects of working in her "office" a former *LensCrafters* store:

Dena: We had our psychologists working out of there for assessments, speech working out of there for speech pathology, attendance services—We set up little desks in the LensCrafters…You know, we just set up little office spaces. One thing that was really odd was the mall opens at 7:00am but the stores don't open until like 9:00 or 10:00. It was completely dark. …We were right across from the food court… [and] it had a play area for kids. They pumped in fake children's laughter.
Amber: Oh God. [Laughs].
Dena: I know! So we were sitting there in this LensCrafters looking out these big glass windows at this darkened play structure with fake kids laughing.
Amber: That sounds like a horror film.
Dena: And it was on a loop. Every 4.5 minutes or something it was the same laugh track. It was really interesting when we would have big meetings in LensCrafters. We got so used to it we couldn't hear it anymore, but then we would see everybody else looking at each other and we'd go. "Oh yeah". And it would be loud, it would interrupt, you know. So weird.

Later in December Paradise High would transfer to the former Facebook building and in January PINT would take over an empty OSH store. Cedarwood Elementary was still standing and could eventually welcome its own students back; Pine Ridge Elementary was damaged, but reparable. Some of the special education programs would meet at the Silver Dollar Fairgrounds in Chico. Honey Run Academy would first move to the Chico Boys and Girls Club Teen Center, and then continue distance learning with support out of the Chico Mall. PUSD also signed contracts to put schools in churches in both Oroville and Chico.

PREPARING THE SCHOOL SITES

Jake Timm describes the role of PUSD Director of Facilities, Maintenance and Operations as keeping everything in working order, "from underground to the tops of the trees." Before the Fire, his job entailed managing all aspects of the physical plant, ordering all the District's supplies, and supervising a team of four skilled maintenance workers. After the Fire these responsibilities expanded exponentially. When I asked him how he got it all done while also navigating his own personal losses, he explained that he was grateful his wife could take care of the insurance claims and other recovery efforts at home: "I didn't have time for that. There was no way I could do that. I needed to be here. I needed to make sure that we were going to get back up and running." And after Michelle made the decision to keep the PUSD open, "It was just not a lot of sleep."

One of the first challenges was getting his team into Paradise, which was currently closed to entry and patrolled 24/7 by a contingent of the US Army National Guard. Someone gave Jake a Pacific Gas & Electric (PG&E) pass to enter town, which he quickly replicated:

> I went right to Costco and bought a color printer so that I could start printing off those so that we could get up into town quick. And I even had one of my [relatives] that lives in [another city], he was with the [specific agency] here patrolling so that made it a little easier to get in. But once we got those PG&E passes then we could get in.

They could now begin readying the four schools that had survived so that they could eventually welcome their own students back. Jake explained the particular emotional salience of these campuses: "It gave the kids a sense of somewhere to go that was somewhat normal…The kids were scattered throughout the county and there was no sense of normal for those kids."

The Fire destroyed the most of the PUSD vehicles, so Jake's team rented three, 26-foot U-haul trucks. They gathered all the cleaning supplies they could find in Paradise and Chico, and began the cleaning and decontamination process. Jake explained what this looked like:

> I got all the custodians and everybody that was still around this area together, and we all came up here and started emptying classrooms…We had a method where the desks would come out, somebody would spray it down, and sanitize it and it would go in the truck…That way when we moved it back into that classroom it would come back off the truck, we would do it again and it would go back into the classroom.… We just kept doing that, and eventually we got all the schools up and running which was just a miracle. I don't even know how we did it to be honest with you. It was such a blur.

Once the buildings were safe and clean, the teachers were able to enter and make decisions about what they wanted moved into their new school sites. Reiner helped develop a communication system involving green, blue, and red tape: Teachers placed green tape on items they wanted moved to their new classrooms in the other cities, and red on items they no longer needed. Then a second round of teachers would come in and replace the red tape with blue for any items they wanted to take. *Two Men and a Truck* then transported everything to the new sites. This seemingly clear-cut system turned out to be surprisingly complicated. Reiner recalled:

Two Men and a Truck did all the moving, so that had to be scheduled. ... but various sites weren't going to be available at the same time...It was this maze where this [school] has to move in order for this [school] to be able to go into a place. [For example] the junior high had to get completely out of the junior high and over to the high school in order for the elementary to move in. At the same time, the high school teachers who were in some of the rooms the junior high were going to use, were going to have to move to other rooms. And in those rooms the furniture had to be moved around. ... It took a while to figure all that out. So you kind of have to look at the layers there. And what's your staffing? You know, how can we group that? You know. I worked to have the high school people meet with their staff to figure out how they could coordinate with the custodial staff to move the furniture to where it needs to be, to vacate the place so the junior high can get moved over, and those buildings so the elementary can then move into the junior high, that kind of thing.

Jake's team also spent a lot of time buttressing the infrastructure at the schools in Paradise. He had to work with PG&E to reconnect power and make sure all of their equipment was phased correctly when they reconnected the power lines, coordinate with the gas company to make sure that the gas lines were operational, work with the heating, ventilation, and air conditioning team to get those systems back on line, organize the installation of water purifiers (since Paradise water was highly toxic), and so much more: "Toilets, floors, roofs, you name it, we had to check it all. So it was a lot of work. We spent between 12 and 16-hour days, 7 days a week up here trying to make sure that everything was ready."

Additionally, the Fire was followed by major rains. This would amplify the damage if his team couldn't protect the exposed areas quickly: "I mean we were in full-blown winter right after the Fire, so it was just making sure that everything was going to function and not be destroyed if it didn't already get destroyed in the Fire."

In some ways it was easier to prepare the new commercial sites that would be housing schools. Those sites were independently owned, so their landlords were responsible for their own repair and maintenance. Jake needed to coordinate some of that, but for the most part his job at these sites involved obtaining the furniture and other supplies that the teachers would need, and supervising renovations required to comply with the Americans with Disabilities Act.

The Teachers and Their Classrooms

It is important to remind the reader that most of the teachers moving into these alternate sites were currently living in trailers, tents, and motels, or bunking with friends, relatives, or other PUSD employees. These big classroom moves happened at a time of major personal instability and grief. This quote, from PINT science teacher Cynthia Smith, illustrates the common experience:

> We were in Redding [83 miles away from Paradise] for two weeks…and then the kids and I went to a coworker's basement [in Chico] and stayed there for two weeks so that we could deal with FEMA and all that craziness. So that was where we spent time…before Thanksgiving…and then we had to eventually go back to Redding so that we could start figuring out where we were going to stay for a while, 'cause yeah, it was just too tight. Luckily somebody from our friend's church had a house that they weren't using because…it was like their vacation home. And so the six of us eventually went there in December and we stayed a couple months up there in Redding. So, it was just so unstable until then, you know, living out of a bag.

The initial moves into the new school sites would also be the first of many more over the next months and years. Three-and-a-half years after the Fire, Tom Taylor offered Pine Ridge Elementary as an illustration:

> Pine Ridge teachers have moved over and over and over again after the Fire …For example, when we came back [to Paradise] we moved the Middle school to the High school, so the High school and the Middle school were sharing facilities. It was the best we had. It was the best we could do. Our two elementary schools combined, the one that burned down and the one that partially burned down, they combined. They were at the Intermediate school….Ridgeview [high school], the school that burned down …First of all they moved down to the Fairgrounds…Then they moved to the elementary school and they stayed there for two years. We got their school rebuilt and they're moving again. If you think about it, it's not as intense as moving your home, but you're moving a thousand square-foot classroom. You can get a lot of stuff in a thousand square feet. Most homes are two thousand. It's almost four years down the road, but the impacts haven't left. And I think that's a statement to the *grit* of the people in our area. Once again, the impact of teachers. You know, we moved the teachers so many times. We work well with the teachers, I think, but you'll hear them joke about, "Oh well. We moved from OSH [Orchard Supply Hardware]. This is still better than OSH!" Or something like that, and they'll laugh about it.

FINDING THE STUDENTS

While the sites were being prepared, PUSD was searching for its students. The District utilized multiple forms of communication to get the word out, including Facebook posts, media coverage, and regular calls to parents' cell phone numbers. Michelle remembered:

> It was just using multiple forms of communication. Somebody may not have a cell phone, but somebody else does. Or they have a Facebook, or they can

go to the library. So you use every means you can…There was no written communication as far as sending anything through snail mail, because nobody had an address that worked anymore anyway. You use the television reporters. They become your best friends. And that's another thing; my job was to develop relationships with television reporters and print reporters so they wanted to help us, and wanted to be with us.

Michelle credits the PUSD teachers with the lion's share of the work of bringing the children back:

The teachers are the ones who really did a lot of the work. They called every family. They sent notes to kids, "little love notes", I called them. They called. They said, "We want you." The teachers are the ones who got down into the trenches to get the kids back…I can't give them enough kudos because that's where the kids needed to be.

The PUSD team estimated that only about half of the students would return when they opened the new schools. But they were also committed to keeping all of the teachers who wanted to stay. The senior administrative team decided the best course of action, for both emotional and practical reasons, would be to team teachers up in classrooms. Michelle explained:

Tom and I knew we had an abundance of teachers, and not children…We said, "What do we do?" And we talked about making very small classrooms of six or seven or eight kids. And then we said, "Why don't we make classrooms of 15 kids and put two teachers together, and have them support each other and be with each other?" We got the president of the union involved of course, and he said, "That's a fabulous idea." And so we went with it. It was all about, how do we support them? And we knew that you get more support when you aren't teaching autonomously, when you can have that other person with you.

Some of these Paradise teachers who wanted to stay were temporarily living in other states or far-flung parts of California. Many of them would end up choosing to commute very long distances, but others took advantage of online learning. As it turns out, Paradise USD pioneered many of the remote teaching strategies that the rest of us would embrace when Covid-19 hit the following year. PINT science teacher Cynthia Smith told me what she was thinking at the time:

Everybody was everywhere. I was in Redding. And I was like [laughing], please don't make me go to work right now. Like, it's an hour and a half drive, you know, to two hours, depending on traffic.

Reiner remembers the PUSD response to these geographical challenges:

> I pulled [the teachers] together and said, "Look, this is what we're gonna have to do. You guys have been experimenting with Google classroom....It looks like this is a direction we're gonna go. I need you guys to imagine how you would do school this way. Let's pull together a plan. Put your heads together, figure out what you need, because...this is your responsibility...I had a teacher that was in Nevada...You have people who are living with friends, or temporarily out of town...or getting a trailer and living on somebody's property. And just making sure people are connected with services...You just kind of pull together a page of resources so that people can get connected to the resources.

Despite this flexibility, many of the teachers did not make it back to Paradise. And those who did come back had varying needs and levels of loss. This raised many questions about fairness and equity. Michelle recalls many difficult conversations shared with Tom and David. All of these were stressful, but many were very sad:

> A lot of our time was spent talking about staffing, the sad stories of staffing. "So-and-so left. They're not coming back. They just picked up and they're gone." [And we responded], "Okay. Let them out of their contract. Of course let them out of their contract. And they get paid for the rest of the year." I mean, [we discussed questions such as, "How many days off are we going to give people?" Well, let's talk about the people that lived in Chico and didn't have a house burn down and the people whose houses are gone. Let's talk about who wants what, who needs what. Does somebody need six months off the rest of the school year? Let's see how we can make this work. So those were very *sad* stories. And we went through every single staff member by name, and there was some sadness when we did that. We bunched that up so we weren't taking all the staff members [all at once] because we just couldn't do that. It was just too traumatic.

Reiner described some of the logistical aspects of these staffing problems as a "Gordian knot" to be untangled. There were many layers to be considered, and many stakeholders to be consulted:

> It became a contract issue and I had to sit down with the union. And we had to look at how many hours people work. What are the required minimum hours for students? What are the hours for teachers? And figuring out, moving forward, how do we adjust the daily schedules to get the minimum required hours and minutes for kids without violating union contracts? What a Gordian knot that was...It was all that more difficult because not everybody had uniform days in the chaos that followed. And so some days had to be lengthened, and some days had to be shortened. And then trying to work that out so that the buses can deliver kids and pick them up. That was a major puzzle. That took some serious time to get worked out.

BEHIND THE SCENES

Michelle, Tom, and David were a very public presence during all of this preparation, but they also worked in very close quarters in their makeshift office in Chico, courtesy of the Oroville Adult Education Career and Technical Center. Here, convening meetings simply meant shifting their chairs and adjusting their computer screens:

> *David:* We were this close together [indicating very close]. Tom sat in front of me. But literally my screen is right here. [indicating very close]. I'm behind him and he would open the screens and that's how we'd talk.
>
> *Tom:* David would say, "Tom, can we meet?" And he would move his computer screen.

When I asked Michelle to describe their leadership process behind the scenes, she explained that one essential practice was the morning "T-up".

> *Every single day* we would start with "What's going right? What do we need to look at?" ...Every morning we would T-up, and then we'd say, "Ok. Let's go!" And so it was all about keeping things moving ...I took it from collective bargaining sessions when we would T-up. Because we did collective bargaining like that. We T'd up every single morning: "What's your goal? Okay. How do we do this?" And so much was coming in for people that I had to put a principal on that: "You're the thank you note person" and "You're the person to inventory and make sure--" because you had to be very careful of the finances. Teachers were starting *GoFundMe* pages, and if they were doing it through the District there's certain laws. There were a lot of legal things we had to get people involved in too. And then it got down to the nitty gritty of FEMA, Cal OES [California Governor's Office of Emergency Services], and the logistics most days. It depended on what the topic of the day was.

As more and more of the PUSD's immediate practical and logistical needs were being met and District was secure, Michelle, Tom, and David were able to start addressing some of the collective trauma in a systematic way. Michelle explained:

> We were saying, "Okay, now we feel the need to bring in different groups." Like all the food servers, all the custodians, all the bus drivers. The big thing was the bus drivers. We spent a lot of time and energy [thinking about them] because they were the first responders for the kids. The bus drivers were *very* traumatized. We spent a lot of time saying "who do we

bring in?" We hand-picked people to bring in and talk to different groups. …Like, who's going to be best for coming in and talking to bus drivers? Who's going to be best coming in and talking to a group of teachers, or a group of food service people, or custodians? We just wanted to make sure that we individualized every case. That's really what our meetings were about, is how to…let people come together and swear, cry, say the District sucks, say *whatever* without any fear of *anything* happening to their job or anything…We spent a lot of time about "let's develop a relationship with the union so that people feel safe to say what they need to say, without fear of losing a job or pissing anybody off. Because this isn't about us. And they need to do that."

The superintendents also came up with policies regarding time off after the Fire. In this respect everyone in the District would be treated the same, regardless of whether or not they lost a home in the Fire. Michelle recalled:

I think we ended up with…fifteen days paid leave to go out and do things. They needed more…That was one of our most difficult things to work through, because you have to draw a line somewhere on the amount of time off people get. That was difficult, and you can't make everybody happy. But that's not your goal. Your goal is to make everybody as okay of a person as they can be internally.

Michelle also set in motion a policy whereby PUSD staff would be able to attend to the myriad personal details involving insurance inspections at their destroyed homes:

My first decision without school board approval I made was, if you have to go talk to a fire inspector, or when they're on your property, go. Just go. Walk off and go. If somebody calls and says they're on your property, you're allowed to leave. Then I cleared it through school board later, which was bad, but you know at that time [inspectors] were already starting to come up. Inspectors were already on people's property, and [the PUSD employees] had a right to be there. And so I'd say, "Go. Take the day. Go." And Tom and David and I always agreed on that.

FEEDING THE STUDENTS

"Everything is Figure-outable." A wooden sign with this phrase currently hangs above Director of Food Services Tanya Harter's desk in Paradise. She coined it after the Fire, and it has since become her mantra. In the early days after the disaster, the only certainty was that every day would present new challenges. The only way to be successful was to remain organized, flexible, and open to unconventional ideas. Tanya's colleague, Food Services Site Manager Linda Shields, appreciated this about her supervisor:

> It seemed like you had to take every day as a new day. It's a new experience because things were not the same as they were yesterday. Flexibility is a key point here, because we had *nothing*. So you have to be flexible…Tanya, she researched every possibility.

One of the early questions was how to feed all of the children who were newly homeless and scattered across Butte County. The PUSD could not do anything for the students who had moved to other areas of the state or to other states. The first plan was suggested by Vince, Tanya's former boss at Chico Unified: "We need to open up some of our kitchens like it's a summer food program." Normally, feeding students out in the community is only permitted during the summer, so they would need special permission for this. The California State Department of Education Nutrition Services Division readily signed off on this plan, which would permit PUSD to use the food they had retrieved from their freezers to feed the children where they were. The PUSD used all available channels to advertise that this would be happening. Locally-based service groups like the Red Cross also helped get this information to families.

Less than a week after the Fire, Tanya's team had established community-based food service for all PUSD students. Paradise community artist Jess Mercer described what this looked like:

> Oh gosh, yeah. They were like a *brigade*. You'd just see all these lunch ladies with their little hair nets, 'cause they just never took 'em off. They'd just be driving. There's all these ladies just driving. It was – I hate to reference it, but it was kind of a *funeralesque* brigade, but you knew it was for something *good*, that they were reviving life. They weren't going to say goodbye to anyone.

And it wasn't just food that they were offering. Jess went on to describe the love that accompanied these deliveries:

> The way I love art is the way lunch ladies love food, [big smile] and serving and helping and making sure that children are okay. So the lunch ladies formed a lunch lady pact, that they would do *anything*. So they lined up all of their own personal vehicles and they loaded all of their trunks with all kinds of food and they went to all the sites. They went to all of the places where our people were [living], like the Silver Dollar Fairgrounds. And they just showed up. And then [a PUSD lunch lady named] Nadine reached out to her quilting community, and then all of a sudden all of her friends made all of these quilts. And then now there were quilts in the trunk. Nadine is the queen of trunk giving. Like, she created trick-or-treating out of the trunks where she lined

up all the lunch ladies and gave out healthy snacks and non-healthy snacks. But mostly healthy snacks – she'd really want me to point that out! And so it was just like, what matters right now? What *really* matters right now? Food. Comfort. Communication. Togetherness.

BUSSING THE STUDENTS TO THE TEMPORARY SCHOOL SITES

PUSD lost 17 busses on the day of the Fire, but they still had plenty left to safely transport their reduced student population to the new school sites. The District did have to get creative about the bus routes. Michelle recalled:

> We had to do this whole giant, wall-long bussing matrix. [We asked families], "Please let us know where your child is, because we need to set up bus routes, and we need to cluster kids so we can set up bus routes." And parents were clamoring for that because all the people were coming back saying, "Is there any way that you can bus so-and-so from here and here and here?" And we were just bussing all over to get them to be with their friends. Our bussing costs were out of this world, but it was worth it for the emotional well-being of the kids.

The PUSD bus drivers were some of the most traumatized PUSD employees, so it is not surprising that many chose not to return. Bus driver/bus driver trainer Chris Rinesmith and bus driver Angie Van Blaricom came back. Chris's home in Magalia survived, and it happened to be nearby one of the remaining schools, Cedarwood Elementary. PUSD stationed a bus there, and starting in early December Chris used this to transport students from Magalia and Stirling City to and from school. She added a colorful welcome sign and seat-belted a three-foot teddy bear onto one of the seats. She fueled up at a commercial gas station called "Chuck's Place." A second bus, driven by Kevin McKay, was added a few weeks later. Eventually routes expanded to the Chico and Oroville areas. Some of these early routes serviced families who still had homes, but students on other routes had experienced more loss. I asked Chris to tell me what that experience was like, she said this:

> When I'm driving the bus going down toward Chico, I look up in that interior mirror and see all those faces, and every kid on my bus had lost a house. They lost their stuff. It just makes you want to try harder to bring them happiness and not sweat the small stuff. They're making a choice to go to school so they're winning, you know. This is an important task to get them there and get them back and make a positive effect on them. That was important, you know, we needed it to happen and we needed to do the best we could with what we had.

THE FIRST DAY BACK TO SCHOOL

The first day back to school for many of the sites was December 3. Michelle described her experience at the Bird Street location of Paradise Elementary, but you can imagine similar scenes all over Butte County:

Michelle: I was at the Bird Street school in Oroville. [California State Superintendent of Public Instruction] Tony Thurmond was there the first day, too. We were serving breakfast together on their first day. And I think I spent most of that morning with tears just running down my face because it was *packed*. Parents were crying, kids are crying, busses are pulling in. It was an *unbelievable* feeling to see these kids come back, and their parents, and—and—I'm going to start crying now. I can't even *tell* you the feeling to see kids come back and have some kind of normalcy. And to see all their teachers out there. The teachers made a tunnel so the kids could walk through the tunnel and see their teachers…That was one of the most emotional days. Our attorney came to that, our attorney whose been part of us, and she's bawling. And if you know our attorney, she never does. And she's just turning her head away. It was probably the most emotional day, other than graduation, I had- was that tunnel the first day back. And the kids and the families showing up.

Amber: So that was the first time you had seen all of these efforts come to fruition?

Michelle: All the teachers were making the calls, and this was the first time I'd seen people back. It was the first time we were back, and Tony Thurmond was just blown away. He said, "If you ever need a job you tell me!" And I'm like, "Yeah, no." And I mean it just was –I kept saying, "The teachers did this. The teachers did this." And they had fixed their rooms up. They had been there for *days*. And it was – It was beautiful.

FEEDING THE STUDENTS AT THE NEW SCHOOL SITES

When the PUSD opened their new school sites, some aspects of feeding the students got easier. But there were still many logistical challenges. For one, only 18 of PUSD's 40 food-service staff returned, supplemented by eight new employees. Second, the schools were spread across a fairly large geographical area. If Tanya wanted to visit all of the schools it meant traveling 106 miles round-trip. She tried to do this at least once weekly to connect with her team face-to-face and offer both material and emotional support. It was important to keep tabs, as 35 of her (formerly) 40 food services employees lost their homes on November 8. They were doing all this extraordinary work to feed students while also undergoing extreme personal stress. Second, there were some things that only Tanya was allowed to do, and this took extra time. For example:

> The town of Paradise was blocked off all the way up to just the bottom part of Magalia. So the families that were stuck up there, they could still go to school up there. But my milkman couldn't deliver up there. My vendors couldn't deliver food up there. But I was able to. I had a special pass, so I became a food delivery person twice a week. I was able to get the food up there.

Tanya and Vince retrieved the warming ovens, garden bars, prep tables, and utensils from the PUSD kitchen, and this was a boon. But Tanya recalls permanently injuring her thumb since it was just the two of them "loading these giant ovens into this little teeny truck." Now they needed a kitchen to put them in. The technician who serviced the PUSD dishwasher happened to know a retired firefighter who had a catering kitchen in Chico. They were able to rent this using insurance money. It was centrally located, and very near the OSH and Facebook schools—in "just this perfect little spot." Tanya still didn't have anywhere to store food, so she opted to use Chico USD's menu for K-8. Chico also loaned her two delivery vans, and a small office space that she and her secretary could work out of.

The Food Trucks

One of the many creative ideas the PUSD Food Services team came up with was starting their own food truck. It started at Paradise High School, which had been relocated to the former Facebook building at the Chico airport. Some folks had begun inviting commercial food trucks to the site, even though the District was already providing free meals. As Tanya explained, eating this way is expensive (about $10 per meal), but the Paradise High School community just wanted to give their kids a "special treat every day." She continued, laughing, "So then I had to get competitive!" The PUSD lunch ladies decided to create their own food truck. They borrowed an unused one from Chico Unified, and opened for business: "Hey!", she told the students, "We're a food truck and we're free!" The truck was fairly nondescript, but colorful. Tanya described their marketing strategy:

> We actually created some different recipes to compete for the kids! What are they walking over there to get? And what can I make and put in this food truck to keep the kids coming to eat with me? I couldn't do the milkshake and the

donut. But we created double stack hamburgers. We even brought special containers for the French fries. They weren't fried because I can't fry, but it helped out a lot. And it made the kids feel special. We still offer the double-stacked cheeseburgers on our regular menus.

The lunch ladies provided much more than warm, nutritious meals. They offered a warm and familiar maternal presence also. The children were sometimes uncomfortable at their new school sites, but lunchtime was the same as it had always been. Food Services Site Manager Linda Shields explained a regular experience during breakfast or lunch service:

> There were quite a few times where [the students] would just break down and start crying. Just their day wasn't going right, or they weren't comfortable at their new school site. And when they were there to get their lunch, they would give a hug and say, "Thank you so much" and [tell us] that this is what they remember doing during a regular, normal day.

Linda also cherishes some of the small homemade gifts the students offered to their lunch servers:

> We got quite a few little posters, you know, thank you posters for doing all the extra hard work just to bring them their lunch. They were very thankful.

LOOKING BACK

The amount of work it took to establish the new school sites and bring the PUSD family back together was staggering. Everyone interviewed for this book worked very long hours on very little sleep, for many weeks, while also managing considerable personal trauma. Yet, they were uniformly reticent to highlight their own efforts, preferring to discuss the amazing things their colleagues did. Case in point: Jake Timm refused to sign the waiver to be featured in Ron Howard's 2020 documentary, *Rebuilding Paradise*, because he felt the attention was disruptive to his work[1]:

> Every time I turned around they were in my way. Every time I got in the middle of something up here [in Paradise], I would get called down there for some bullshit meeting that had nothing to do with anything that I was working on. They were totally disrupting our work ...they were hampering the duties that I was trying to accomplish at that time for the greater good of our town. I found it very distracting.

---

[1] Most would agree that *Rebuilding Paradise* is a wonderful documentary, and it has received many awards. Jake's point is simply that he could get more done without the cameras.

Jake agreed to be interviewed for this book only because he already knew Jess Mercer, and other local connections vouched for us. But mostly he welcomed the opportunity to help others facing disaster by sharing what he had learned. When I asked him to sum up his experience of preparing the schools for the students and teachers, he shifted the focus to his community:

> I was hired for a job and it was an unexpected job. We just did what we had to do to adapt and overcome, and that's what we've done. You know, we're a proud little community and that's just the way it's always been and it's not gonna change. It's gonna be different, but it's not gonna change. The core people that are still here have the same mentality.

Later Reiner would tell me that Jake "worked himself into pneumonia." And when I complimented Reiner on being "a rockstar" (Michelle's words), he also shifted the focus to the people of the PUSD:

> It's amazing to me what we got done under the circumstances. And it's a testament to the people, you know. It's a testament to the people we work with… Invest in your staff. You invest in them so that they are a strong team, and they believe in themselves, so that when you come across and say, "Okay. This is the next thing. I know this is difficult. I know this is hard. This is what we need to do. I'd like you, to the best of your ability, to tell me how this will work best for you so that we can make it happen." So with them having some of the power, and having a say, being kept in the loop, you know, and being able to say, "No. I can't do that." But yes…they stepped up to the plate. I mean… the majority did. This happened because everybody felt they were making an important contribution.

REFERENCE

Howard, R. (2020). *Rebuilding Paradise* [Film]. National Geographic.

CHAPTER 5

THE SCHOOL IN THE HARDWARE STORE

It's an Ace Hardware now. I still walk into that building and go, "Oh, Barbecue. Sixth grade." I do, you know. Yeah, it's just how I see that building. If I need a flashlight, I'm going to go to seventh grade science. It will always be that way for me in that building.
—Reiner Light, Camp Fire Educational Coordinator

It is strange, Paradise teachers and staff told me, to shop for plumbing supplies or a new hammer in aisles that used to be their classrooms, or to pay for one's items at one of the two check stands that used to serve lunch to the kids in those classes. It is amusing to purchase a plant or some potting soil where your students used to eat lunch or play games during physical education Yet, some Paradise Unified School District (PUSD) employees do this routinely at the Westlake Ace Hardware in Chico, California.

This Ace started out as an empty Orchard Supply Hardware (OSH) store, and for one very difficult and meaningful semester after the Fire, it served approximately 200 students as the temporary location of Paradise Intermediate (PINT) School. This chapter offers a portrait of this extraordinary school, which would eventually be given the affectionate and ironic nickname, "POSH."

HOW IT STARTED

PINT School principal Larry Johnson has had a remarkably accelerated administrative career. After graduating from Paradise High School (PHS) he served 4 years in the Marine Corps, and then returned to Butte

---

Educating the Phoenix, pages 71–81
Copyright © 2026 by Emerald Publishing Limited
All rights of reproduction in any form reserved.
doi:10.1108/978-1-80592-429-620251006

County to teach social science for 5 years. When the Fire happened, he was the newly-minted assistant principal of his alma mater, PHS. After the Fire he helped guide the school's transition to the Chico Mall, which included working with Jake Timm's staff to remove and clean furniture, and running the hybrid and distance learning program from the mall storefront. When PINT principal Reiner Light moved into the Camp Fire Educational Coordinator position, superintendent Michelle John O'Neal invited Larry and his colleague Cris Dunlap and serve as the coprincipals of PINT. Larry was a bit surprised by this offer, given his relative lack of administrative experience. Nevertheless, he was still a Marine at heart. He knew he was needed and readily accepted the challenge.

POSH Was Not Posh

The POSH team had to move fast. Once the lease was signed, they would only have a few days to transform an abandoned hardware store into a functional school. Unfortunately, the POSH site was arrestingly filthy. Michelle recalled her teachers' first reaction: "The teachers rebelled a little when they first saw how dismal the space was, but then of course rallied around each other and the building and moved mountains to make it work."

Teachers, custodians, and administrators at all levels pitched in to help transform the space. Michelle remembered:

> The amount of cleaning we all did in the four days before we opened cannot be overestimated. I have no idea how much cleaning supplies we used, but it was a lot! We laughed and cried while we cleaned and truly wondered how we were going to set up an environment to make kids feel safe.

A clean store was still not a school. So many other problems and questions remained. Larry recalled some of these:

> How are we going to get TVs going for lesson plans? How are we going to charge the students' Chromebooks? How are we going to be able to do *anything* in modern day education that you do? You know, what is this going to look like?

In an early example of the ingenuity that was to come, Larry and Reiner grabbed a drill they found lying around and began using it to identify which electrical outlets worked. Surprisingly few did, which seemed ironic for a hardware store. They chalked this up to routine safety procedures during the store's closing, but it was concerning. The Internet had also been disconnected. The team worried it might take months to get online, and in a situation with so few other teaching resources (everything back in Paradise was burned or contaminated), the Internet seemed especially necessary.

However, things started looking up as Larry and Reiner brainstormed how to organize POSH for learning. Larry explained: "We were walking around and we just figured it out—people could set up their classroom areas in aisles. I could set up an office in an aisle!"

And that is precisely what happened. Each day for an entire semester, approximately 200 sixth, seventh and eighth-grade students, around 20 teachers, and several administrators and support staff conducted their workdays out of OSH aisles, checkstands, and other customer service areas. This was an entirely new way to do school, but Larry was certain of one thing:

> The philosophy I developed at the very beginning was, I don't know what this is going to look like. I don't know what's going to happen. All I know is we are in a massive building. We're in a very unique situation and we need to find a way to do something unique. We need to walk away from this having done something absolutely huge.

Here is what that huge thing looked like.

THE SETTING

Readers can experience POSH for themselves on YouTube, thanks to a 16-minute documentary titled *From the Ashes: A Paradise School Documentary* (Kessler, 2019). I recommend pausing here to view this short film before reading on. Otherwise, it is fairly easy to get an idea of what POSH looked and felt like by imagining any large hardware store. Your local OSH, Lowes, Home Depot, or Ace will do. You enter the automatic glass doors at the front of the store. Picture the colors; in this case mostly white, gray, beige and green. You are greeted by one of the coprincipals who is watching the door, or by the POSH office staff, who are set up at the Customer Service Center. You sign in and pass through the checkstands. You see two Lunch Ladies cleaning up after serving breakfast out of checkstands Five and Six. The students, about 200 of them, have just left the large area in the front of the store after their morning assembly. You are sorry to have missed the assembly, because you've heard these are very encouraging. After the pledge and announcements, the principals acknowledged a couple of student birthdays, and a teacher gave awards to a few kids who had demonstrated good character. Everyone felt lifted up and connected to this strange, wonderful community.

Now listen. There's so much space to carry noise, so many hard surfaces to reflect and amplify sound. Those 200 students are now dispersed around the building. Remember the din of your own middle school cafeteria at lunchtime? This is twice as loud. Think about how you might learn science or math or language arts in the midst of all that noise and activity. Consider what your voice would feel like if you were a teacher trying to be heard. Imagine the headache you might have.

Now empty all the store's shelves, except for about twenty aisles which are being used as classrooms, offices, and supply storage. These aisles are double the width that you are used to seeing because the small custodial staff has removed shelving in-between to create larger spaces. Teachers are calling these "double-wides." There are also cardboard partitions on the end caps to create some semblance of contained spaces. Say hello to the Counselor in her aisle. She has arranged it carefully to be as calm and relaxing as was possible. There's a soft rug on the floor (which helps with noise reduction), and bean bag chairs for "a little chill zone for the kids." An experiment with a punching bag has been abandoned, but it was there for a while. She has placed her books, her computer monitor, and other important materials on the former product shelves. Principal Larry Johnson has also reserved some seats in his aisle office for students who are having an emotionally tough day, or who are in trouble. (These two things tend to align.) Overall the effect is cheerful and homey.

The teachers' aisles are a wonder of creativity. They are decorated with colorful craft paper, educational posters, inspirational messaging, and dozens of plants. Some teachers have white boards; others write on large sheets of paper stuck to the shelving. Table lamps and strings of Christmas lights help warm the glare of the overhead florescent lighting. Shelves have been lowered to create desk seating along the sides, or raised to create standing desks. Books and other donated or newly-purchased educational resources line the other shelves. Each classroom has a cabinet full of Chromebooks, and a $500 silent electronic generator that recharges batteries overnight or during lunch. Some aisles even have a TV that runs off of this generator. Wi-Fi repeaters have been placed strategically to create hotspots. You notice that there are two teachers in every aisle, paired up for mutual support and to keep everyone employed. Many of these teachers are wearing T-shirts with positive sayings printed on them. You notice that these teachers speak into head-worn microphones linked to headsets worn by their students. This lets them speak in a normal voice and still be heard easily. This recent innovation has been a game-changer.

Off to the side of POSH you notice the Garden Center. It's been cleared of all its shelves so it can serve as the main PE area. You see a several students gathered around ping-pong tables, and a dozen more are running around playing games. They are careful to avoid the students doing gardening, making ink from local trees, or working on a large-scale project about rainforests. Go a little further and you'll be at the warehouse in the back of the store. You've found the other PE area. There are two basketball hoops.

Orange netting along the sides contain the balls. A couple of students are riding their bikes there, and a few more are zipping around on scooter boards. If you go all the way to the back of the store you will find the POSH Teacher and Staff Lounge located in the room where OSH retail employees used to take their breaks.

A TYPICAL DAY AT POSH

A typical day for coprincipal Larry Johnson started at 5:00am at his home in Chico. He checked emails while he got dressed. After giving hugs to his family, he left in time to arrive at POSH around 7:00am. His goal was to get there before anyone else, but his "early bird," seventh-grade history teacher Tracy Parks, sometimes got there first. After arriving he'd do a lap around the entire building to check for safety issues. He often encountered unhoused people sleeping around the perimeter. These folks had been in the area for a long-time; they were not Camp Fire refugees. Larry would ask them to please move along and find another place to sleep. Then he would set the alarm for the day and turn on the lights. His maintenance crew of one to three people were usually the next to arrive, followed soon after by the rest of his teachers and staff. Everyone would greet each other warmly and then find their aisles to start their own morning preparations. Larry's office was also in an aisle, but coprincipal Cris Dunlap set up her office by one of the two glass entry doors. The other door was near the Customer Service Center, and this was coopted by the POSH office staff. This meant that each door had someone posted there for security. The POSH did have a few surprising guests, and this was disruptive but also amusing.

> *Larry:* People would show up to shop and just walk in.
> *Amber:* That would happen?
> *Larry:* Oh yeah. All the time. We'd be like, "Oh, sorry, man, this is a school right now." And they'd be like, "Huh?" Some people would think you were joking, and they would just keep walking. And we'd say, "No, no, really. Look around!" And then they would look. And you would see this look on their faces as they realized there's kids everywhere.

On the first day of school the POSH staff had absolutely no idea how many students were going to enter their doors. Everything was fluid. Larry recalled:

> We didn't have them registered for classes... We didn't even know for sure what teachers were going to be able to come back, which ones had moved out of the area or not moved out of the area. So they just landed.

When students arrived each morning, they congregated at the front of the store near the cash registers. The first few days back, POSH started first period with a 5 or 10-minute assembly that included the Pledge of Allegiance, birthday shout-outs, and announcements. Getting everyone together was helpful for community-building and comradery, but it also helped orient students, teachers, and staff to what came next. Larry recalled: "Kids were confused, 'Like, where am I supposed to go?' We didn't have a schedule locked in at all. Everyone was confused. Including us."

These short assemblies gradually increased in length because, Larry said with a smile, "I'm a bit of a talker." These longer meetings still included the Pledge and announcements, but they became much more meaningful. Some of the POSH teachers knew about a character-building program called *The Virtues Project* (Popov, 2000), and this became the focal point of these morning assemblies. The virtues are a set of 600 positive attributes (think gratitude, commitment, and service). Students learned about these virtues, practiced them, and were acknowledged individually during the assemblies. These Virtues Assemblies worked so well that PINT (now renamed Paradise Junior High, but that's a story for later) still does this every Monday and Friday. For example, at a recent assembly four students were given awards for demonstrating respectfulness.

POSH decided to build their new bell schedule around these morning assemblies, but of course they didn't actually have bells; much like college courses, teachers used their own methods for determining when classes began and ended. When the morning assembly dismissed, students and teachers dispersed to their aisles and began learning for the day.

THE POSH TEACHERS

One of the many things to appreciate about POSH and PUSD generally is the quality of its teachers. Before the Fire and afterward, their administrators maintained absolute confidence in their professionalism, dedication, and creativity. The administrators' role, therefore, was to support the teachers emotionally, practically, and financially, but to leave the pedagogical decision-making in their hands. Michelle explained this during her interview:

> Our teachers are so creative that you don't micromanage anything their doing. Instead you marvel and you visit and you say, "What do you need? What can I get you? How can I help you?" You know, my role as superintendent [places palm on her heart], was, "just tell me what you need." ...I didn't have to be creative as far as the classrooms, because I couldn't touch these teachers with a candle. I mean, they are just so good, and I just marveled at what they did. I just provided resources and got out of the way and let them do their thing I had to stand back and let them go.

Michelle's assistant superintendent, Tom Taylor, echoed this sentiment while also adding that the teachers were working with very little in terms of material resources:

> The teachers were extremely creative...The teachers had *nothing*. All their curriculum was up in Paradise, and they really couldn't get most of it because it was damaged, contaminated or whatever. So the teachers were doing whatever they could...And honestly the teachers were still in a space where they were, I think, in shock. I know they were because I talked to some of them. We all were. Not just them. And while they were trying to rebuild their lives, they were trying to get supplies to serve kids, which is just incredible since the majority of our staff were displaced or they lost their homes.

The teachers were also a strong source of support for each other. Larry was impressed by this characteristic of his staff. When I asked for an example, he told me about one of his PE teachers:

> The leader of that in my mind was Mike O'Connor, who's still the PE teacher, and he is a master teacher, and even better human. He was there for everybody every step of the way and would go out of his way to help anyone and everyone. And it was leaders like that that made it happen. It wasn't administrators, and no offense to any administrator, but it was the *teachers* that were there for their friends and their colleagues, and they were the shoulder for other people to cry on. They gave them a hug when they needed a hug, or they told them some stupid joke to make them laugh when they were about to break, you know. So it was people like him that stepped up so much that –I know me, I couldn't. I wouldn't have had a shot without the staff there, leading one another.

The PE department was an important and unique support for the students too, largely because PE provided an outlet to run off some energy, and a chance to get out of the noisy building to do fun things for a while. Larry explained:

> My PE department was a very, very strong team. Very strong team. And I struggle to see how we would have gotten through this experience without that department because they gave kids that break, that thing that they needed, and all these experiences, and took them all over the place. They thought so far outside of the box.

Some of this out-of-the-box thinking resulted in field trips. The three PE teachers used PUSD buses to take students outside 2 or 3 days each week. They often played games at outdoor parks, but on one notable occasion the students visited an *Urban Air* trampoline park. The other departments took full advantage of local resources too, often using the Chico public buses to do so. Larry estimated that the POSH students went on "well over 50" field trips during their semester in the store. For example, they visited local museums, California State University Chico, and a daycare center. Larry recalled the daycare visits:

> There was a daycare for really young kids within in walking distance. We actually did a field trip over there with the leadership kids a couple of times. The kids went to the daycare and played with little kids, which they absolutely loved. That's something we couldn't have done up [in Paradise].

Class time inside POSH equally imaginative. For example, a history teacher determined that it was possible to make ink out of a local species of tree that was abundant around POSH, so he taught his students to prepare the ink and write with it. One clever history teacher created an in-situ lesson on environments by challenging his students to learn about their new school. We can see this in the following vignette from the *From the Ashes* documentary. The teacher, Dan Owen, is speaking animatedly to the students in his aisle:

> We're not talking about islands or deserts though! Our environment we've been learning about is our new school. And so this school here in this warehouse is an environment. Naturally in a warehouse, especially one that used to be an OSH building, there is lots of shelving. And so we've adapted it by turning it into standing desks, sitting desks—
>
> [A student interjects inaudibly, then Mr. Owen continues]
>
> Yeah! The Office is in a customer service area, right? That's not a usual thing!
>
> [Another student raises her hand and gives an example]
>
> Excellent! [Mr. Owen points to the shelving] All of the ends of these aisles had plastic caps that you'd put the price tags in. And we cut them into meter sticks so you guys could use them for science. You used them to measure this environment, find out how long our new school is, how wide the school is, how far it is to the bathroom, etc.

This kind of problem-solving became a hallmark of the POSH semester. History teacher Tracy Parks noted that many teachers found treasures tucked away on shelves or in the back room that could be repurposed for learning. Others used common items in nontraditional ways. For example, science teacher Marc Kessler noticed that students were spending free time flipping water bottles, so he created a bottle flipping lab where students had to fill their bottles with different amounts of water, precisely measured, and then flip the bottle 15 times at each volume. They recorded their results on a data sheet. In an amusing example, some teachers used a rogue shopping cart to transport paper or other materials from the supply aisle to their classroom aisles.

Because of their teachers' resilience, creativity and dedication, the POSH students grew in their academic knowledge, skills, and dispositions during their time in the hardware store. Yet, the PUSD teachers and administrators I interviewed always emphasized that the most important thing after the Fire was addressing the students' social and emotional needs. Academic progress was secondary, as it had to be. Traumatized children have difficulty learning. Therefore, the school's main success was its community. More than anything, Larry explained, the students and teachers "just wanted to be together." Recall from Chapter Four that the students' families were given the option to send their children to regular schools; the PINT parents chose to send them to POSH instead. Larry remembered:

> I mean the fact that even one kid would go to school in a hardware store instead of a school that was probably much easier to get to is just remarkable. The fact that so many kids reunited and came back, and parents would literally drive hours away just to get their kids to school to be with their teachers... I had one family, I can't remember where they were staying, but they drove two hours each way to get their kid there.

LUNCH, CHECKSTANDS FIVE AND SIX!

PUSD Food Services Site Manager Linda Shields and her colleague started each morning at the rented commercial kitchen in Chico. They would pack up that morning's breakfast items, load them into the back of a truck, and drive them over to POSH. Their first stop was to check in with the office staff at the former Customer Service Center at the front of the store. Meals were served out of checkstands Five and Six. After breakfast Linda and her colleague traveled back to the commercial kitchen, prepared the lunch items, and returned to POSH for the afternoon meal.

In a time of so much change, it was important that the food be familiar. Students would have four or five choices for lunch, including things like pizza, deli sandwiches, hamburgers, taco bowls, and a garden bar. The options would rotate each day. Students would line up at the checkstands, collect their meals and some encouraging words from their Lunch Ladies, and then take their food back to their improvised cafeteria, which consisted of plastic tables set up near the OSH warehouse area. Afterward they would be released to the former Garden Center for supervised recess.

The sharing of meals has deep cultural significance all over the world, and at times it can rise to a sacred act. During her interview, Linda explained that serving meals at POSH was healing for both servers and students alike. During her interview, she explained that the students seemed very grateful to have something "normal" in their school days. Other than being served at checkstands, breakfast and lunch were much the same as before the Fire.

The students also seemed to understand that the Lunch Ladies were doing extra work to prepare and serve their food, and they were grateful. Linda found all of this personally therapeutic:

> To think that you're there to feed these kids that are all homeless. And just to make sure that they're okay, and to give some normalcy…Of course, you're going through trauma yourself…It was helping me that I could help them find some stability.

After lunch the students returned to their aisle classrooms for the afternoon's lessons. At the end of the day, Larry and other teachers and staff went outside for bus duty. The students boarded PUSD buses, or drove home with parents. Some sixth-graders stayed for an optional homework club. Other students were stranded at school for many hours while their parents dealt with Fire-related concerns, like housing or insurance issues. Larry would leave with the last of the students, typically at 6:00 or 7:00 in the evening. He'd hug his family, eat some dinner, and respond to more emails before bedtime.

LOOKING BACK

The successful POSH experiment finished at the end of the spring 2019 semester. The school marked the occasion with a special promotion ceremony held at Pine Ridge Elementary in Magalia. This was the first time everyone came back together inside the burn scar. The next fall PINT School moved to its next temporary location, PHS. For the next two years PHS and PINT shared this space. However, in March of 2020 PUSD pivoted yet again, this time to distance learning. In a district that had already been through so much, COVID-19 was an especially hard blow. Paradise was perhaps better prepared than the rest of the country, however, in that they had pioneered distance learning a year earlier while they waited for their alternate school sites to be ready. The following year (2020–2021) the PINT students started back to their PHS campus 2 days per week. This kept class sizes small to minimize the spread of the virus. The final transitions happened in 2021; PINT students initiated an idea to change their school's name to Paradise Junior High School (PJHS). Their initiative was supported by parent and staff feedback, and approved by the school board. The PJHS students are now back at school full-time in their beautifully updated and restored junior high campus.

If the ordinary things that make up our daily lives have memory, then the Westlake Ace Hardware in Chico, California is a fulsome repository.

Its former students made a fieldtrip there after the store reopened as Ace. Larry described the experience:

> It was really fun to watch and to talk to kids about it and the staff, and to see just the look on people's faces even. They're like, "Wait a minute. Wasn't this Mr. Kessler's classroom?" "Wait. This was the sixth-grade area? There's barbecues here now!" It was really fun to see that. And then to watch the kids tell stories to the other kids that weren't there. "Oh, yeah, this is how this works." And we'd be looking at each other, and we're like, "Man, did we really do that?" Like, "How did we pull this nonsense off?." And then [the Ace staff] had all the kids sign this poster that they had professionally made. And it's still up.

It reads:

> *This building proudly served as the Middle School for the Paradise Unified School District in the spring of 2019 after the Paradise Fire. Ace Hardware in Chico is Proud to be part of your community.*

REFERENCES

Kessler, T. (2019). *From the ashes: A Paradise school documentary* [Short Film]. Tava Kessler.

Popov, L. K. (2000). *The Virtues Project educator's guide: Simple ways to create a culture of character.* Jalmar Press.

CHAPTER 6

EVEN HEROES ARE HUMAN

> *Even heroes are human.*
> —Tanya Harter, PUSD Director of Food Services

Thus far our main focus has been what the Paradise Unified School District's administrators, teachers, and support staff *did* to keep their students safe and their District alive after the November 2018 Camp Fire. We began the morning of the evacuation and escape, and concluded with the establishment of the new school sites in December 2018 and January 2019. This chapter shifts the focus to aspects of what these heroes *felt* along the way. The title comes from Tanya Harter's interview; she summarized this chapter perfectly.

THE THREE-LEGGED STOOL

The "Three-legged Stool" refers to the senior leadership team of Paradise Unified School District (PUSD) superintendent Michelle John O'Neal and her assistant superintendents, Tom Taylor and David McCready. In the early days after the Fire, they began using this metaphor to describe their interdependent leadership style. It is a warm term of affection that remained meaningful even a year later when Michelle retired and Tom took over her position. Indeed, the three friends still use it fondly today. Michelle explained:

> We always called ourselves "The Three-legged Stool". We'd go around like this all the time: [Michelle makes a gesture with two fingers and her thumb to approximate a stool]. We'd kick one leg out and make jokes, "We're falling, we're falling! You're not here." So we'd make jokes like that.

Michelle, Tom, and David's individual strengths had always complemented each other, but this mutual support became even more pronounced and necessary after the Fire. For example, David McCready's job description made him the go-to person for figuring out how to pay for what the District needed, but after the Fire some of his personal attributes came to the fore. As Tom explained in his interview, David's family roots outside of the Town of Paradise made him an important person to lean on when objectivity was necessary in post-Fire decision-making:

> Gosh. David was such a critical piece...Michelle and I were pretty close to it, obviously...My town of fifty years burned down. Michelle's town where she raised her kids burned down. But David, he was pretty critical, and still is critical in this whole thing. ...He was probably sometimes more rational than Michelle and I were in his processing of things. I mean he was really critical.

Michelle's master's degree in school counseling likely helped set the tone for their senior leadership meetings, which included some proactive strategizing about maintaining their own mental health. With so many people looking to the "Stool" for support and guidance, they could not afford to fall apart. When I asked Michelle to describe their coping strategies, she listed three. First, they made it a point to check in personally with each other during the day and in the evenings. She told me: "We just checked in to make sure everybody was okay. And we'd check in at night. 'Did you sleep last night? How are you doing? Go to bed.' We took care of each other that way."

Second, the three superintendents looked to their spouses for support. These folks provided a soft place to land and a fresh perspective. The partners also took on a larger portion of the normal household responsibilities and personal disaster-related problem-solving. Indeed, this was a common theme among all the PUSD employees we spoke with: They felt empowered to work on behalf of their students because they had family willing to take on more than their usual share at home.

The third coping strategy they agreed on was that they would abstain from alcohol use. Michelle explained:

> We promised ourselves we would stay away from alcohol because we know that's a depressant. And David doesn't drink anyway, and Tom drinks very little. I'm the one that probably drinks the most of all of them. And we said, "Hey, no alcohol because we know it's a depressant and we're not going to go there."

A SENSE OF HUMOR

The three superintendents have an enduring friendship that acknowledges both deep wells of anguish for the loss of their town and also laughter at the absurdly comic situations in which they found themselves as a result. Humor was also invaluable for helping keep these leaders going even in the very worst of situations: Recall the story of David and Tom fleeing their town after making sure all the schools were empty. This was an objectively traumatic event. Yet, Tom chose that moment to point out to David that his "hair product was failing." This seemed genuinely funny at the time, and it remains so whenever these friends retell the story. Michelle also remembered a comical story about finding Tom's truck after the Fire:

> It was probably three weeks or so after the Fire, and Tom had said, "My truck is at Ponderosa [Elementary]." Because he had to get out and run across fences through the Fire. And I said, "Okay, let's go check it out." And so we go, and he gets out and he's like, "Oh my god, it's *perfect*. Nothing's wrong with it." And he puts his code in and he gets in. Well I had walked around the other side, and I started yelling "Don't start it! Don't start it!" [laughing] The other side was *charcoal*. That other side – I'm like "Don't start it!" I'm laughing, I'm cracking up so bad. So he gets out and he walks around and he's like, "Oh my god!" [still laughing] But one side of the truck was perfect. The code worked to get in. The electrical worked. The other side was *charred*. And that's when people go like, "they *laughed* over that?" We were laughing so hard and it wasn't even funny.

Michelle explained the therapeutic value of these belly-laughs:

> Humor was a *huge* part of what we did. People probably at times thought we were irreverent because we *had* to laugh. We laughed a lot. And maybe over things people didn't think were funny, and probably weren't funny. But you know, we had to laugh…It was the only way we could get by.

Humor helped other PUSD employees navigate the disaster as well. Paradise Elementary fourth-grade Teacher Vicky Steindorf evacuated her home while listening to the Talking Heads song, *Burning Down the House*. Director of Food Services Tanya Harter joked that the reason she and her colleagues didn't quit after the Fire was that they didn't want to "look like assholes." Paradise Intermediate Principal Larry Johnson found it amusing when random people walked into his school—a former hardware store—to buy a hammer or some electrical tape. None of these situations are *actually* funny, and the storytellers know this. But laughing in the face of sorrow reduces stress, provides temporary relief, and allows one to access a new perspective. It also helps bring closeness and feelings of social and emotional connection. The PUSD team desperately needed all of these resources during the acute stages of the trauma, and they are still benefitting from them now. Personally, I (Amber) can attest that my family finds it hilarious that one of the only things to survive on our property was a plastic lawn flamingo. We eventually christened him "Phillip," and we all agreed that the next house should be built from whatever Phillip was made of. As I write this story now, I feel sadness and joy in equal measure.

CARING FOR ONE ANOTHER

One of the most consistent findings from our interviews with PUSD employees was the degree to which they felt cared for and supported by their colleagues and administrators during the Camp Fire recovery. The teachers were the main source of consistency and support for the students, but of course they were also dealing with their own tragedies. As Bus Driver Trainer Chris Rinesmith put it, "Everybody was broken. Everybody was broken and you were trying not to cause more damage by being less than professional. It was a hard situation for everybody." Michelle and the other senior leaders recognized this:

> You can't forget to take care of the teachers when you are so busy taking care of the kids and the families, because it's all one big family. There's a book out, it's called, *If You Don't Feed the Teachers They'll Eat the Students*.[1] That's a very true statement.

When I asked Michelle to tell me what taking care of her employees looked like, she highlighted both emotional and practical supports. Of emotional caregiving, she said this:

> It looks like making sure you take the time as the leader of the District to call, check-up, and bring them together. Food is so important in our society. Make sure you have food and coffee. Make sure they can get together, especially site-level, so they can do their crying and they can do their hugging. That's what I mean by taking care.

With regard to practical supports, Michelle emphasized how critical it was to offer time off from work so employees could take care of problems associated with their personal losses:

> We gave them the time off they needed, which was very difficult. What saved us is that different people needed different time off. And we had lost so many kids that we were able to buddy the teachers up ... and put two teachers in

---

[1]Connors and Streams (2000).

each classroom so they had the support of one another. So if one teacher was feeling like they were going to break down or had to get out of there, they could. So that was a really good decision, I feel, to give each peer support physically and emotionally.

POSH science teacher Cynthia Smith truly appreciated having time off to figure out housing for her family:

> The administration was completely understanding about not being able to be there. It was more about making sure that there was at least somebody there [in the classroom] to help, obviously. But with so many teachers who were homeless—I mean seriously, we were *homeless*.

Cynthia's colleague, POSH history teacher Tracy Parks, concurred. She was grateful to work for the PUSD instead of one of the nearby districts:

> I was teaching in [nearby] Gridley twenty-something years ago. I thought, "Oh my gosh, if I were still teaching in Gridley, it would be hard to take time off to go meet with the [insurance] adjuster or whatever." ...There were a lot of teachers living up [in Paradise] who worked in other districts. They didn't get the benefits that we were able to get, because our district gracefully gave the teachers fifteen additional days to deal with everything. And at the time I thought, "They don't get any of that and they've got to be at home at 1:00 to meet the adjuster or the banker, or whatever. Ugh."

Tracy and Paradise Elementary fourth-grade teacher Vicky Steindorf were also grateful for their administrators' empathetic stance, as this excerpt from their interview demonstrates:

Vicky: I think that something that the administrators did try really hard to do was support teachers.
Tracy: I felt well supported.
Vicky: With counseling, yoga, massage chairs in the staff room, things like that.
Tracy: And a lot of them lost houses and things too, so I felt bad for our admin. A lot of them were going though what we all were, but then they had the added responsibility of trying to hold it all together.
Vicky: I think that for the most part they did a good job continuing to give support. I think that was crucial for the rest of us to keep trying.
Tracy: Right. They had to make sure that they were leaders and captains of the ship.
Vicky: But be compassionate about it.
Tracy: Oh yeah, definitely. I felt like, "Okay, they know what's happening so we're good." You know? That belief that they were all good up there in their position, so we just do what we're told and we're good. I felt like that even though it wasn't that way, because they didn't know what was going to happen next either.

PUSD Director of Food Services Tanya Harter told me how she tried to support her staff, too:

> You could tell when somebody was having a really rough day. You know, they're in a trailer. They need a little motivation to make it through the next meal serve. I'd just pull out a little gift card and put it in their pocket. "Hey, why don't you to go buy a pair of jeans?" or, "Get some shoes," or "Buy your blender." Get them thinking about something other than what they were feeling. Those were some nice little ways to motivate people.

These small kindnesses could only go so far. Tanya described a sad situation where two former lunch ladies quit their jobs on their first day back on campus:

> They were rock stars. I had so much fun working with them. They were displaced in Oroville, so I had them go to work at Paradise Elementary, the school that we housed in Oroville. The first day that school opened, the press was there, the governor was there. All these people were there. And I had a kitchen full of people. I didn't need that many people in that kitchen, but they wanted to come to work. So my one gal came to work. She stayed through lunch, and she called me that afternoon and resigned. She said, "I can't do it. I can't see those kids." She and another gal, they both just resigned. They were like, "I see my grandkids in those flames, in every one of their faces." That's how I lost a few people. They tried. They just couldn't do it.

Another unnamed PUSD employee told me a difficult story about one of the people they supervise:

> There were a lot of really tough times for some folks. I had one [employee], who suffered a lot with depression, and she was stuck in her trailer with her teenage [child], and they had to share the bed, and they had a dog and it was raining all the time, and there was just mud everywhere, and it was just hard. And she was suicidal. And that put me in a different hat. Like I don't have that hat. I didn't know what to do for this person, I mean I quickly figured it out. I called our [supervisor] because we've had several meetings about how to deal with some of these things that were coming up…It's a different hat to have to put on for sure.

Financial Stress

For some PUSD employees, financial stress exacerbated the Camp Fire trauma. The District kept all of their people employed, which was a godsend, but life was so much more expensive after the disaster. Not everyone had cash reserves or room on their credit cards to meet the immediate financial need. Moreover, not all insurance is good insurance, and unfortunately many Paradise residents found this out after-the-fact. Further, it is not uncommon for people on the Ridge to live in paid-for houses that were passed down from a previous generation. Some of these homes were uninsured. Some renters didn't have rental insurance. All of this impacted some people's ability to be resilient after the Fire. PUSD Director of Student Services, Dena Kapsalis explained:

> We see that our most fragile and disenfranchised or marginalized members of our learning organization, whether staff, teachers, or families and students, are the first to experience symptoms of loss or symptoms of that trauma, whether it's learning loss…home loss, or the loss of, as Schonefeld[2] would say, their "assumptive world"…Those families that have fewer resources available to them, whether financial or family or support, or just being able to continue to maintain a certain sense of normalcy. The Fire exposed a lot of ground in terms of destroying the vegetation and structures, but it also exposed a lot of gaps in services. Sort of that symbolic exposure. It's interesting how it does that.

After the Fire almost everyone had to find a new place to live, and this left some PUSD employees more vulnerable and exposed than others. For example, many people suddenly had to travel long distances to work, and gasoline is notoriously expensive in California. Paradise Elementary teacher Vicky Steindorf explained why this was a problem:

> We lost staff because they couldn't afford to drive to Oroville. They didn't have cars anymore, or the car that they had couldn't reliably get them there. We lost several of our staff that needed their job! They just couldn't get there. They couldn't afford the gas or they didn't have a car anymore.

Camp Fire Educational Coordinator Reiner Light saw this. He described how the District responded to the need:

> When you get a janitor that's driving from Red Bluff [one hour away], who can barely afford gas and whose car is, you know, questionable—They're thinking, "Why am I driving to Chico for work when I can barely make ends meet?" In that case we tried to look after them. I went to the superintendents, and asked a board member if we could give them some cash cards. I said, "These guys are really hurting for gas money. This has a big, big impact on them." Those kinds of things seem so small, but they end up being really big because it's hard on their morale… So just making them feel like they're heard and that their concern can be met.

From the beginning the PUSD leaders knew that they would also need to call on experts to support their people. Their employees were grateful

---

[2]Schonfeld et al. (2002).

for this. POSH science teacher Cynthia Smith remembered one of these interventions:

> They did so much for staff. They had an art teacher come in and do art classes with us [smiling]. I still have my snowman that I made. We did one for the high school. Any grade who wanted to come in to do the art could come in. And so the high school had a bobcat that they painted, and the middle school had the snowmen. It was just really nice that people were coming in, and administrators were saying, "Yes please! Help us take care of our staff."

When I asked bus driver trainer/bus driver Chris Rinesmith what helped make her job easier after the Fire, she told me about a psychologist the PUSD hired:

> The school district employed him. And that was really generous of the school district to get some help for all the employees and so we would meet with [him] maybe once a month and then maybe once every couple of months. We'd have some group sessions where he'd talk to us, and we'd just round table it and we'd all share some things. Because it was traumatic what we went through, of course. It was nice that the district cared enough to do that. So that was a thoughtful thing for them to do, and necessary as well because we have to be well if we're trying to take care of kids who are traumatized as well. That was a good thing.

TEACHERS AND STAFF CARING FOR EACH OTHER

Another finding from our interviews with PUSD teachers and staff was the significant degree to which they supported each other. This took many forms. First, they experienced an unprecedented solidarity, a unity of purpose, and at times, a willingness to meet catastrophe head-on together. As an illustration, consider what Vicky Steindorf said to her teacher colleague the morning of the Fire as they evacuated four students and a dog out of town: "I said to [my colleague], 'There's no guarantee we're getting out of this, right? You realize that. And so we're going together because we've been best friends for this long. If this is our last day, we're going together.'"

Even teachers and staff who had not been "best friend" close before the Fire experienced a deep sense of community afterward. Food Services Site Manager Linda Shields explained:

> My team and I got very close. There weren't very many of us left after the Fire. We were a group of, I believe, 28? Now we were down to 14. So we're all pretty tight-knit. [Director of Food Services] Tanya was always there for us. Absolutely every day she was there for us.

Linda pointed to her daily carpool as a major source of mutual support for the lunch ladies:

> The commute with my coworkers every day helped. It felt like a sense of closeness. You could talk about things, and it would help healing while trying to go about your normal day. Because none of us wanted to leave home. We didn't want to leave our homes.

This sense of closeness and community that began prior to the Fire, and deepened afterward, remains today. When I asked Vicky Steindorf and her colleague Tracy Parks to elaborate, they said this:

Vicky: I feel like this was an older staff in our District. Many of us had been doing it for a while, and it was a pretty close group in each of the schools. I think there was a closeness among the teachers. For example, I still have a chat on my phone that is our Paradise Elementary family. We're not at the same schools anymore. Many of us aren't even in the same district.

Tracy: We do too, for Paradise Intermediate. And some of them are even out of state now.

Vicky: Right. And we still, if something is happening with this person or you know, a baby was born, or whatever, like "I got a new puppy," there is still a lot of communication. I think the experience of that closeness was, "I'm not leaving. I'm not leaving her back. You know. She's coming in, I'm coming in." Do you think?

Tracy: Oh yeah.

Vicky: I think that was a big piece. Not only are we not leaving our students, we are not leaving each other.

Second, many of the teachers and staff who did not lose homes voluntarily took on a larger share of the workload as a way of taking pressure off colleagues who had big losses. Cynthia Smith recalled: "Many of the teachers that were trying to find a place to stay, like me, we didn't do as much. And the people who *did* have homes, they took over for us and supported us."

Vicky Steindorf called this a "community of closeness":

> It was hard. I mean you just didn't know what each day was going to bring. Whether it was a student falling apart, a teacher that was falling apart, an insurance company that called—You were allowed to go see your property and so you sometimes left in the middle of the day to go do that. And somebody is stepping in to cover your class or cover your position. It has been a community of closeness I think.

Third, many of the PUSD employees who did not lose their homes opened their doors to colleagues and friends. Assistant superintendent David McCready had two trailers parked in his driveway for months. Vicky Steindorf had ten people living with her. She found this to be therapeutic:

> That helped me a lot actually. My house tends to be a meeting place for my friend group who are all teachers ...And then the Fire happened. We had four cats and three dogs. Each of our bedrooms had a family living in it. Our office space had a family that lived in it. We took turns cooking. It was the perfect time. I mean, how lucky was I that I got to – [begins crying] offer that space to those people? Because they were a lifeline for me too, where I could go to work every day and be positive. I also was diagnosed with cancer, so I had all of this stuff happening. It's hard to support others when it takes a lot of you from you all day. And then you go home and you're like, "Okay. I can lay on the floor with this other dog and someone else already has dinner made." And that made such a difference be able to go, "Okay. I can do this."

CARING FOR THE STUDENTS

The PUSD administrators, counselors, and teachers understood that their students would not be successful academically unless they addressed their social and emotional needs first. In the quote below, Michelle explains the stance she took with regard to PUSD curriculum in the first semester after the Fire:

> Let's do our art. Let's do our talks. If they want to write, they can write. Let's read our books. Let's get our bean bags. We've got to take care of their social and emotional needs. These kids, right now they're hurting. They're traumatized. As are you guys [the teachers]. And academics will come later." So whether people agree with me on that or not, I did not put academics anywhere near the front.

Cynthia Smith described what this looked like from her vantage point, teaching science at POSH:

> [The administrators] put academics to the side. They did not push us to go back to the textbook. They just said, "Come up with some activities so that these kids can learn at least a little bit while all this is going on...And so it was really nice with Christmas because there's always so many fun activities you can do around Christmas time. It wasn't about being lenient or anything. They were just understanding... Everybody was just so understanding, because we were going through the same thing. We didn't overload the kids. We didn't have them do more than we knew that they could do. And we put academics second. We needed to do that for ourselves too.

Most teachers took a proactive approach to dealing with student emotions. Below, Vicky Steindorf explains how she started each day of fourth grade at the temporary Paradise Elementary campus in Oroville. She also laments that the students who moved to other districts did not receive the same care:

> I started every day with "Our Checklist for Today." Students could mark things like, "I feel like I need to see a counselor", or "I need to sit by myself today". Those kids [who moved to other districts] didn't get that. They didn't have a counselor that was right there if they were falling apart or saying "I need to know where my mom is." You know, we would call on our cell phones to try and get their mom, because the child just needs to say hi…Kids would come back to us and say that they were in Chico or wherever and they just were lost. People didn't understand. They'd sit there and cry and [the teacher] would be like, 'Okay open your book to page 45. Finals are next week. Let's go." And the kids are like, "Ughhh"' Our kids were together. Those other kids were lost. Ours had someone who had the same experience. That was a big piece too, I think.

Vicky also acknowledged that her boundaries with students remain softer than they were before the Fire. She is more likely to attend their birthday parties, for instance. She also describes herself as being "more personal" with the new students she works with in her post-Fire and post-Covid-19 role as an E-learning teacher:

> In the past I think there was much more of a boundary between "I'm Mrs. Steindorf and you're my student. We have a job to do together." Now I'm much more personal. I say "I love you" to my kids. I hug my kids. I talk about things. [For example] I found this really cute reindeer. Tomorrow I'm going to Zoom from home so that my kids can see what my little reindeer looks like and what my Christmas tree looks like. I wouldn't have shared that before. … I was always there for them. They knew "I am here to help you."…But I'm there in a different way now.

Vicky has also become more vulnerable with her students. In the following quote she explains how this vulnerability manifested when she was in treatment for lung cancer:

> I talked to [my students] about what was going to happen next. Because I wasn't sure–I had a pretty aggressive form and they were going to have me start chemo really fast and I'm going, "I can't just not show up for my kids. I want them to know why I'm not here." I wanted them to know, "When you see me I'm not going to have hair" and "What do you think that might feel like? How would that be weird?"

Vicky's students responded by being more vulnerable themselves. She smiled as she told me about how some of her young football-player students responded to her diagnosis:

> I had the little football boys. After they found out they came to school in pink shirts and pink socks. And football is a thing in Paradise. And these boys would drive me crazy. They were kind of punky, bully boys because football is big here in this community. But they were like, "Okay, this is a different game. This is a different vulnerability." That's the thing. I'm more vulnerable with them, definitely, in my teaching. And I let them be more vulnerable.

The teachers I spoke with also made a deliberate effort to focus on positive aspects of their experience, and when possible, to orient their students toward the positive. This wonderful dialog between Vicky Steindorf and Tracy Parks illustrates this:

> *Vicky:* I'm going to say something that's totally crazy. I wish it didn't happen, but I'm not sad I did go through it.
> *Tracy:* I agree.
> *Vicky:* I'm a better person. I feel like I tend to be a pretty empathic person anyway, but I'm glad I was with those kids. I'm glad I was sitting in that car [evacuating with my colleague]. One of the things I think about all the time is, how can I spin this to be positive? Whatever it is that's happening. I mean there were a lot of good things that came out of me having cancer. There were a lot of good things. I've learned you can live with only one lung. There's good things, right?. [Because of the Fire] I did not have to move 27 years' worth of classroom stuff. That was my positive. I mean I ended up at a new school, but I did not have to pack up all those boxes and move all those things. Am I sad about some of the things I lost? Absolutely. My grandmother's Alabaster bowl…and wicker baskets she brought back from Egypt—Am I sad about that? Yes. But, the rest of it was stuff that I would have had to pack and I would have had to go, 'Do I really need this? … And Tracy has some of that same experience with a big house with lots of things you stored and kept and you didn't have to move it.
> *Tracy:* We had a big three story house full of stuff and my grandparents' stuff from before they died and blah blah blah. And just stuff. Kids' stuff. You know, I didn't want to get rid of it and it all burned to the ground. And it's like, 'Well, I don't have to move it!' [Laughs].
> *Amber:* Do you think the [students] were able to catch some of that positivity from you?

Vicky: I think so. I think a certain group of the kids wanted to be around that. There was so much sadness and people dwelling on the depressing side of it. I think some people, kids that are like me, gravitate to the happy side of things. Like, "Okay. I don't want to be around that. I want to be around something more positive. And what can we look forward to? And how can we laugh about the situation that we were writing on shelves with holes in them and you have to move your paper so your pencil doesn't poke through. You know how the little metal shelves have those little holes. There's always something good that can come out of each day.

Tracy: Yes! Right! When I was creating my Aisle 12 classroom—the paint aisle at POSH—I made sure that I was putting up sayings and phrases that mirrored that. The kids, a lot of them were sad and depressed and it's like, "No no no. We're okay. We're here. We've got each other. Here you want some food? We got some food. It's all going to be okay."

Amber: Where did you get that attitude?

Tracy: I don't know. I just—

Vicky: That's why we are teachers.

When I asked these teachers what made it possible to maintain this positive stance when working with their students, Tracy was quick to respond:

Tracy: Oh, that's very easy to answer.

Amber: Okay.

Tracy: Knowing that our number one job was to be the best we could be for the kids. And that's when I started buying all these t-shirts with different sayings like, "Blessed" or "It's a Wonderful Life," and wearing them trying to show the kids this is not the end of the world. This is just one piece of life. We can get past this.

Suspending Standardized Testing

PUSD also pioneered the idea of a district temporarily suspending all standardized testing. In our post-Covid world, this stance does not seem so radical, but when Paradise suggested it in early 2019, it was. Michelle explained:

The teachers were going, "I can't do this [testing]!" And I'm like, "We're not going to. We won't. I promise you we won't." And I had the school board behind me. I had to get [California State Superintendent of Public

Instruction] Tony Thurmond and [California Governor] Gavin Newsom involved here too, because I said, "Our kids aren't ready. I'm not going to traumatize them."

Unfortunately, the law required PUSD to forfeit six million dollars in Federal Title 1 funds if they did not test their students. The District counted on these funds as part of their regular budget, and this was the absolute least optimal time to give them up. Michelle pushed state officials to forgo testing and still let PUSD keep the funds:

> I said, "What do I need to do?" [They said], "It's never been done. No one's ever opted out of testing and got an opt-out." And I said, "What do I need to do?" And they said, "I don't even know!" I said, "Okay. I'm going to make a couple phone calls." So I called Tony [Thurmond's] Communications Director and said, "We can't test! Tell Tony we can't test. We can't put these kids through that. Every parent is going to ask for an exemption and I'm going to support it. I refuse to go to these parents and say, 'Oh by the way your traumatized child now needs to do a week's worth of standardized testing.'" And so it took probably two months of letter writing and getting professional people to back me, professional psychiatrists to back me, and say, "this is not what these kids need." And for the first time ever – now that's changed because of Covid– but for the first time ever they allowed a district to opt out of standardized tests and not get penalized.

In June of 2022, four years after the Fire and just at the tail end of the worst parts of the Covid-19 pandemic, Tom Taylor (who had taken over as superintendent when Michelle retired one year after the Fire) explained the ongoing impact of the PUSD's post-Fire emphasis on student mental wellbeing:

> After the Fire we had to first start addressing everybody's mental wellness. And that goes for staff and students. And I would like to say we're past it. I'd like to say if it weren't for Covid we'd be past the whole mental wellness thing. But Covid just added to it. You know, a big part of our curriculum, a big part of our meetings, a big part of everything we do, is this new thing to us called "mental wellness." We have people doing staff development for our teachers on how to support students who have been traumatized, as well as, how do you support teachers who have been traumatized? How do teachers develop their own skills to help themselves when they're dealing with so much trauma? So much of your focus heads that direction, and honestly it gets away from academics. It's kind of Maslow's Hierarchy.[3] But it gets away from the academics. Covid impacted it too. Covid just added to everything we were dealing with, with the Fire. We were excited to be back

---

[3] Maslow (1943).

in school and we were going to have a normal year. It was a highlight. And then come March, and we tell them "school's closed." So everything has just been added to it. So as a district one of my goals, our goals, is that we are trying to get back to that academic piece and bring a real focus back to academics. But you can't do it without—You know, if you have a child who is struggling from trauma, or the fact that they haven't eaten or something like that, you've got to deal with that first.

"Thank God for Covid"

PUSD Director of Student Services Dena Kapsalis told me that some of the District's teachers who had lost everything in the Fire took it personally and experienced resentment when their students acted out in class. The strange subheading above is a quote from one of those teachers, and it represents a normal and expected response to trauma. Dena explained:

> [These teachers] felt like, "I lost everything. I'm getting my stuff together every day to come teach you and this how you thank me? With all of these out of control behaviors that make my day terrible?" When the pandemic hit...in March of 2020 and we shut down schools, I had a teacher come in and tell me, "Thank God for the pandemic. Because I had nothing in my jar. I was completely empty. I had lost every tool I used to have. Every strategy to work with kids is gone and now I'm just angry at kids." That was a classic symptom of trauma, right? That numbness, anger and sympathy fatigue. All those things combined for [this teacher]. [The teacher] said, "I needed a long, long, long, long break from kids. Interacting with them face to face, I just couldn't do it anymore."

That one teacher was probably speaking for others. So the question was, how should the District respond to these teachers and staff? One way they responded was by having a dedicated counselor just for teachers, administrators and staff. Another strategy was bringing the different employee groups together for their own "healing circles." Dena explained:

> We got one of the guys who organized the County support and he and I brought all of the different employee groups together. We met with just the custodians, we met with just the food services folks, we met with just the teachers, and so on. And we had a full catered dinner with to-go boxes ready, and then handed out all the gift cards we were getting to Target, Safeway, or gas cards. And then he did a healing circle where he did a lot of therapeutic listening for the groups so that they could talk about what they were experiencing...We did that several times. It helped. People would reach out and thank me. People would say, "I'm so glad you guys did that."

WHAT MADE RECOVERY DIFFICULT

During our interviews, PUSD employees pointed out two things well-meaning people did after the Fire that made their jobs more difficult. Fortunately for us, they also offered solutions for handling these problems in future disasters. The first problem was finding time to respond to all of the phone calls and emails from concerned friends, family, and colleagues. The way they framed this problem echoed difficulties some bereaved people experience after the death of a loved one. Dena Kapsalis recalled:

> One of things I found really challenging, and I want my colleagues in other districts to know and hear this, is, "Don't require an answer from me". I'm the director of student services, right? I'm on this hamster wheel of emails all the time. And I really try to get back to people. I really, really do. And if I don't get back to somebody, bing! Three o'clock in the morning, "Oh my gosh! I didn't get back to so and so!" ... After the Fire, I got hundreds of emails from people, which was awesome. But half of them required an answer. "Did you lose your school?" Or, "Tell me what things you need." Or, "How are you?' Tell me how you are." This was really nice, but what I needed was, "I'm just thinking about you. Reach out to me if you need anything from me." Don't require anything else of me. My husband is the one who pointed this out – I'm up at midnight [and he says], "What are you doing honey? Get some sleep." And it's like, "Oh no, the superintendent from [a distant district] just sent me an email...she asked me what I needed. I just wanted to let her know that I'm good right now but thanks though."

Dena went on to explain that the PUSD used this experience of email burden to craft their offers of help to school districts impacted by the massive 2021 California Dixie Fire: "We're emailed our colleagues after the Dixie fire. We did that. But we didn't say, 'Tell me what you need.' Instead we said, 'We're thinking about you. Reach out if there's anything you need.'"

The second thing that made recovery harder—and this was mentioned by pretty much every PUSD employee we talked to—was dealing with the staggering amount of unsolicited donations of material goods. Assistant superintendent David McCready described this problem as "daunting." It created real practical problems, but also added an emotional burden to the very folks the kind-hearted souls were trying to help. When I asked Dena Kapsalis to explain this, she first reminded me of the 2012 Sandy Hook Elementary school shooting in Newtown, Connecticut. Dena had studied aspects of this event through Dr. David Schonfeld's National Center for School Crisis and Bereavement, and she thought it could help illustrate some of what Paradise experienced after the Fire:

> *Dena:* A class of first graders was mowed down by a mentally ill former student who was then an adult. New Town Connecticut lost several teachers, several staff members and 20 elementary students. It was a tiny little school, a sweet little school…I mean, devastating, right? So Schonfeld talks about how within a week of the shooting, the town started getting deliveries of teddy bears from all over the world to show grief, support, and love for the children who had been killed in the shooting. After about the 14th giant delivery truck container full of teddy bears—there were more teddy bears than there were people in the town delivered—The people in the town started becoming physically sick at the sight of teddy bears. They didn't know what to do with the teddy bears. Do we burn them? Do we bury them? They began to be so completely triggered by the teddy bears, and the teddy bears were everywhere. And to this day, they still have these shipments of teddy bears. The thing is, the person, the 17-year-old girl in Ohio who puts her allowance money together and buys the teddy bear and packages it up and sends it is doing it purely out of love, right? So the guilt and feeling sick about the donations is also another plate in the air.
>
> *Amber:* Another burden, yeah.
>
> *Dena:* It's like, "Oh my gosh, oh my gosh. Not another teddy bear." But then you think about this sweet person who put it all together and paid for it and sent it. And then you're like, "I'm such a terrible person because I don't appreciate this." [laughs]. And then it's like, "Ah! But I'm still grieving the loss of these kids." So that's an example of donation fatigue.

PUSD students also received some teddy bears during the holiday season, but these were well-received. The real problems were school supplies, books, and—the real "teddy bear" of Paradise's disaster—backpacks. Assistant superintendent David McCready told me that the District still has more backpacks than they know what to do with, and the Fire was nearly five years ago. Dena explained how the teddy bear story related to PUSD:

> My own personal story about donation fatigue is that first Sunday after the Fire. We were all working 24 hours a day…We had set up a temporary district office in Chico. That's where [superintendent] Michelle was, and payroll. Payroll was still happening. We're trying to just keep the machine going, right?…So I'm getting ready to go in…I'm walking off my front

porch and I see this woman and this man who I don't recognize and they're walking towards me. They're both clutching two or three huge target bags full of things and they're walking up to my front porch and I say, "Oh my gosh, what's happened?" The woman goes, "Oh hi Dena. I'm a teacher in [another district]…and our school just collected a bunch of binders and paper and pens and staplers …and things you need. We didn't know where to take it because your school burnt down, so were just bringing it to you is that okay?" And I'm like, "Oh my gosh! Thank you so much." And then she says, "We've got about six or seven more bags in the car, where should we –?" And I saw that there were already two or three bags on my porch. And I was like, "Oh thank you so much. Oh my gosh, so incredibly thoughtful of you. Yeah, go ahead and put it right here." And I turned around to my husband and said, "Get this shit off my porch like, now." Like, "Get it out. I don't care what you do with it. [Laughs]. I don't – I really do not care." It was just like *oh my god*. And then then of course all the way into the office I'm like, "Ugh. I'm a terrible person. These people put all this time and effort and this is how I refer to that help? Oh my gosh, I was feeling so bad.

Dena was quick to point out that there was a real need for supplies after the Fire, a sentiment that was also mentioned by every PUSD employee we interviewed. The issue was that the responsibility for receiving, storing, organizing, and distributing all of it fell on people who were already overburdened by massively increased responsibilities at work, and often, at home. She explained:

I oversee homeless and foster youth services. I'm the liaison for the distinct. I'm the attendance officer, suspensions and expulsions, and special education, and then anything else that comes our way. And now it's just two of us, me and my assistant, that do all of that because we have lost several employees…We went from five to two. We had a teacher and aide, and then we had a full-time attendance clerk, my assistant and me. So, now we're just two…We also have our actual jobs that we're still having to do…I mean, I liked being involved in the recovery aspect of things, I just also needed to still do my job.

When I asked Dena what she would have had the donors or the District do instead, she repeated something I had already heard from at least four other PUSD employees: School Districts should enlist a donations coordinator whose sole responsibility is doing this job:

Right away a donations coordinator should be established. If it's an admin that's great. But if you can't find an admin to do it, then anybody. That's the person you direct all of those things to. And maybe that donations coordinator is not somebody who's experienced any trauma. Maybe it's somebody from the outside that comes in just to help you. Because money starts rolling in, people start dropping off food, I mean, literally everybody is up to their eyebrows in just everything you can imagine. And so having a donations coordinator where you can say [to donors], "Thank you so much, here's the number or the email of the donations coordinator. They'll take care of all the donations." Dr. Schonfeld is the one that gave us that advice. Get a donations coordinator right away.

Paradise first tapped one of their data clerks to take over the donations, but she quickly "started drowning" because her normal PUSD job had already expanded beyond capacity post-Fire. Camp Fire Educational Coordinator Reiner Light then agreed to take responsibility for the donations. One of his first challenges was finding space for everything:

> We had this little tiny office space that the county had loaned us that probably wasn't 1,000 square feet. That was our district office. And stuff was showing up and piling up. I would have to load it in the truck, and part of my job was going around and delivering this stuff to sites.

He was also meticulous about record keeping and reporting out to the School Board, as there are strict laws about this kind of thing, and doing it wrong could land the District in a lot of trouble with the State. Reiner also tried to write a thank you letter immediately upon receipt of the donation for the obvious reason of extending their gratitude but, also because he would too quickly fall far behind.

Assistant superintendent Tom Taylor also mentioned that it is okay to say, "no" to donations:

> It's okay in a situation like this where people call to offer help, to say "no." And let me start by saying this—One of the amazing and critical things that helped our community is people reaching out to us. Because it gave us hope. And hope is kind of all we had. People would call, and they would want to help out. But the other part of that is, you have to be cautious because sometimes those donations can create more work for your staff that's already overburdened.

Reiner explained how the PUSD handled this after-the-fact:

> We ended up posting, "Please don't send books or backpacks." Because we were just swimming in them. What ended up happening is people cleared out their libraries and sent them to us.... Some of which we could use, and some of which we couldn't. So then I ended up having to sort those.

When thinking about the PUSD response to the donations, Dena Kapsalis believes, "Overall it was handled miraculously well. But there was a lot we learned."

LONG-TERM IMPACT

As I finish writing this chapter, Paradise is preparing to commemorate the fifth anniversary of the Camp Fire. There has been so much growth and so many wonderful changes to the community in the last five years. And yet, I think the people of the PUSD would like the reader to understand that their trauma is still very present. The Camp Fire is not something you get over. Three years after the Fire, and toward the end of the worst parts of COVID-19, teacher Tracy Parks gave her assessment of the students' recovery:

> *Tracy:* The students really are still struggling. I think people outside education might think, "Well it's been a couple years" or "Oh everything's fine.: But I look around and I don't think they're fine. And maybe part of that is COVID. I don't know.
>
> *Amber:* It's hard to say.
>
> *Tracy:* I'm not a psychologist, but I think it's going to be generations before things are normal.

Superintendent Michelle agreed that the trauma still impacts the people of Paradise, even though most of the rest of the country rarely thinks about their disaster. The recovery has been miraculous thus far, but it is far from finished:

> *Michelle:* I think at times [people] don't consider the long-term effects. This is not something that you get over. People are not over it today. They're not rebuilt, they're not over it, they're still struggling. The kids and teachers, I mean they're still struggling mentally and emotionally with all of this. And even myself. You don't think about having Post-Traumatic Stress Disorder until you see a small fire or you smell smoke or something and then just the adrenaline just rushes through you. I think people don't understand. I mean, and this is human nature, so I'm not saying it's bad, but they're on to the next disaster. Because that's how we are. We're on to the next disaster. And *this* disaster will never, ever, be over. Ever. And that's what is hard for people to understand.
>
> *Amber:* Yeah, we've had so many disasters since then. People forget.
>
> *Michelle:* Right. Right. And that's human nature. I don't want people to dwell on it either. But just for the people who lived through it, it will never, ever be over.

REFERENCES

Connors, N. A., & Streams, J. (2000). *If you don't feed the teachers, they'll eat the students: Guide to success for administrators and teachers.* Incentive Publications.

Maslow, A. H. (1943). A theory of human motivation. *Psychological Review, 50,* 370–396. https://doi.org/10.1037/h0054346

Schonfeld, D., Lichtenstein, R., Kline Pruett, M., & Speese-Linehan, D. (2002). *How to prepare and respond to a crisis.* Association for Supervision and Curriculum Development.

CHAPTER 7

EMBRACING RADICAL EMPATHY

This chapter is Jess Mercer's first-person account of her work with the Paradise Unified School District schools. I (Amber) introduced Jess in the first chapter. She created the Ridge Key Phoenix, the 800-pound monument created from more than 18,000 keys from burned homes, schools, cars, and businesses. She is also the founder of Butte County Art on Wheels, a community-oriented mobile therapeutic art studio (See Figure 7.1).

No one can ever prepare you for the moment a drill no longer is a drill and primal survival activates within. No one can prepare you for the gravity that holds you down into reality without room to budge when tragedy hits. Yet, you can prepare yourself to enter these spaces with purpose, poise, and gratitude when called to be the helper.

A call for help may come in a frantically ringing phone as alerts are tripping over themselves like salmon swimming upstream. It may also come in a muted worried nod when you ask someone how they are doing today. The surface pressure around you ready to burst from nothing and everything all at once. At least, this is my experience while working with and through a trauma personally and professionally that made national attention.

For the majority of my adult life, I've worked serving at-risk youth in a variety of settings. I served as a youth counselor in an institutional setting, then jumped into working with group homes and foster care agencies for over a decade. I thought I knew how my life path was unfolding, and assumed I had control of how I shared myself with the world. Yet that was not in cards, and I became deeply ill at 31 years old. Before I knew it, I had

104 • Educating the Phoenix

Figure 7.1 Jess Mercer's *Ridge Key Phoenix*. *Source:* Photograph by Douglas Keister with kind permission.

lost my career, driver's license, and ability to care for myself independently. Taking more than a few steps was my greatest daily achievement. I spent the better part of year convinced my life was ruined, and I would never be "the same." Short of two years was spent in doctor offices, getting tests and relearning basic skills. I had no idea just how useful this lesson through destruction was until I had to apply it outside of myself.

I began working as a part time store clerk on disability two months before the Camp Fire. I was humbled by my physical traumas and the tireless climb of recovery as I stocked the shelves and smiled at customers. The morning of the Camp Fire my alarm clock went off and introduced me to one of the saddest days in my history. Yet, the days just following the fire are notably some of the biggest bounds toward understanding empathy on a grandiose scale many will never understand.

The first call that morning was from my stepmother sounding robotic and frozen in fear as she muttered, "We are coming, we are coming right now." The cryptic and indigestible truth of her statement sunk in as my phone began vibrating from emergency alerts. The sky was transitioning aggressively from a night sky to a black cloak highlighted by red embers jumping miles in the air. Hours passed as I waited for my parents to safely land what is normally 20 some minutes away after their 5-hour drive through hell. I met them in the parking lot, witnessing their first true breath of air in hours, and holding them as the beast continued to fill every crevice of the sky with a black pen. Pulling them inside, I saw their tattered clothing, unbuttoned due to dressing in panic. None of us had any idea how to hold the feelings drowning us individually and collectively. To this day, there will never be the right words to encapsulate the emotions and feelings of the first 5 minutes embracing my family after they fled with only each other and the clothing on their back. My father didn't even have time to put his teeth in. That is how quickly the Camp Fire forced the entire Ridge to vacate or perish.

Now, sitting in my small apartment harboring my weathered parents was my reality. I immediately unlearned that we have control over anything past our present moment. I often shied away from being present, and found myself often unraveling the past and predicting the future. The space in between all that is where the magic is, and especially where the tools to heal can be found in my opinion. The first night of embracing radical empathy and understanding the responsibility of honoring the present moment was pivotal. In fact, it is why I am who I am and why I do what I do. Let me tell you a bit more for context.

The first night my father threw his keys on the table and froze for a moment. I asked him if he was ok, and quickly realized that he was realizing alongside me that his keys may no longer have purpose. The locks, buildings, and items they belonged to were potentially gone forever, and the wait to establish that truth was excruciating. It was quickly apparent that the damage was more extensive than anyone could possibly understand in the first few hours. With that being said, Paradise, California was 95% destroyed, and several surrounding areas were deeply affected as well. Losing 95% of your town doesn't look like a big box store closing and/or the ghostly feel of no human movement. It looks and feels like there is nowhere to touch, feel, or see in the same fashion you could hours before the flames came through.

I realized quickly that the keys represented much more than their intended purpose, and that thousands may be feeling the same sense of loss when holding their own. I knew if I could latch on to a common thread that was woven into the hearts of thousands that morning, maybe I could tether us all back together again. I put out a call for art in a simple social media post with a homemade flier explaining my purpose. I asked for people who desired to rid themselves of their keys to donate them to me so I could create a Phoenix sculpture to gift to the town. Little did I know this project was going to change the trajectory of my life thereafter. It started with a few mason jars set in a Chico, California shop for people to come and safely relinquish their keys. Within hours the jar was full. I amplified my efforts by placing more jars around Chico and surrounding areas. Again, week after week, the jars were full. Before I knew it, people were mailing, handing, sending, and dropping their keys off by droves. Whether it was hope to move forward, to let go, or simply to be part of something bigger with their community, hundreds participated.

I spent days volunteering at local shelters, finding clothing in church basements, and gathering resources for my family and other families scattered fearfully around the area. Thousands of people were displaced in a matter of hours, and some still have not returned since the brave drive that saved their lives. While spending time at the resource centers, working at the shop, and building the sculpture, I became aware of a deep-set gift to assist people through trauma. Some part of my soul is able to shepherd any individual regardless of differences in politics, creed, color, and so much more. Time stands still when every part of you is broken. I felt a calling to do more for my family and everyone I met as the keys came in. The letters about the keys' stories and family memories in the spaces lost were all encompassing, like a million people reading me their autobiographies all at once. I still have all the letters, and I often reread them for encouragement whenever I need a reminder to be present and grounded.

A month after the fire, while working in the retail shop, a little girl no taller than the counter in front of me asked my name. I told her and asked if I could help her. Her response led me to the next chapter of serving the community post-Fire. She asked if I was collecting keys, and I responded with a gentle smile and nod. She reached into the pocket of her dress and handed the tiniest key I'd seen yet. I asked her what the key meant to her. She quietly leaned in and told me the key was to her diary, but now her secrets were gone. I assume when you read that sentence some sort of tenseness or stomach drop vibration came over you. I felt it as well, and I realized the children who survived the fire would need a mammoth amount of support. I realized that in their stages of development this trauma changed everything for them and then some. As the grown-ups were trying to pick up the pieces, thousands of children were simply trying to understand why they couldn't go home. With a comforting smile and thank you soft spoken, I took her small key and put it safely in my pocket.

I thanked the little girl for adding to the Phoenix. (I eventually placed her key front and center under the beak so she could easily find it later on.) Her story and this experience spoke volumes to me. I wanted to do more to help, and knew in that moment the next step was to help the children in my community by simply listening to their present moment. I left work that day and decided it was time to follow my intuitions. I had no idea where to start, but I knew if I found the children I could help the children. I began making calls, setting up meetings with local funding agencies, and asking everyone I knew how to help.

Within two months of the fire, what was left of our student population were blending into shared and abandoned spaces around town. Some schools were placed in a old warehouse that shut down, and students were dancing with manequins in the back room and having class between aisles blocked off by sheets. The image was unlike anything I've ever seen, almost unbelievable. Yet, what I did notice on that first tour of the warehouse is nearly every student was smiling as I walked around. They were simply happy to have each other and be together. I took this as the biggest sign of hope and reality thus far. I knew that bringing people together with purpose was how I could personally serve my tattered community.

I met with a funding agency, called the North Valley Community Foundation, the following week. I inquired how to access funds to support the youth as donors were pouring money into assisting the recovery. The CEO, Alexa, let me know of some small funding options that may work. I had never written grants before, I was not and am not a nonprofit, and I have never been an accountant. All of those barriers quickly went out the window, and with some gumption and a bunch of online research I wrote my first grant to support my community. I found a local nonprofit, the Chico Art Center, to support my goal and allow me to write the grant with their support. They housed my funds while I focused on the outreach. I called my first project "The detachable mural project." I took the same supplies to each school wherever they were located since the Fire and built a detachable mural with each school. The hope was each mural would then transfer when they transplanted back to the Ridge. Little did I know, several schools quickly became few. Some schools have two murals in them today, as they combined the schools when reality of losing 90% of our population became undeniable.

We painted murals in the basement of an airport terminal, an abandoned hardware store, an abandoned school, a local Boys and Girls Club, and so many more places our youth were sheltered. I built 15 murals in 15 weeks, and it bonded me with our school district, charter schools, and homeschools to this day. That relationship continued to blossom in time as it was quickly recognized my mission to serve was unmatched to other efforts occurring. Youth at every campus knew my name, but lovingly called me "Pan" because I would show up when the doors and windows were open to bring fun. I am still called Pan on campuses I serve nearly five years after our tragedy. It is by far my favorite reward thus far, and I feel trusted and seen mutually by the amazing young people I have watched on their journey of recovery.

Youth handle trauma in such a unique fashion as the adults around them attempt to figure it all out as well. Yet, youth don't carry the barnacle of reality that comes after devastation. They are not able to call insurance companies, but they hear their parents passionately do so. They are not able to call lawyers, but they hear their parents do so with confusion. They are not able to get themselves to schools miles away from where they once learned, but they do live the truth of displacement. This is not to say adults did not support youth, but it is a fact adults had extremely difficult decisions and actions to take after the fire. We tend to forget youth may not be part of the logistical parts of recovery, but they are fully observing everything around them. I remember hearing first graders talking about their mommy yelling at the insurance company. Read that again, and ask yourself if this would be a sentence you'd hear in a natural classroom setting. This led me into my second major project to serve youth wherever they were.

After pure success of the mural project, I was looking into the next school year and how to assist best at that point of the recovery timeline. I wrote another grant and called the program "Tap-Pen, Tap-Out." I made agreements with local schools to set up an art booth one day a week on each site. When youth or staff were feeling flooded with emotions on campus, they could come join me and do a 15 minute reset art project. My hope was to catch emotional outpours before youth were sent home, staff experienced burnout, or just to help recenter an escalated feeling. I wanted to serve as an innovative buffer to relieve some of the trauma residue our youth were experiencing as they were still displaced. The program was successful and enlightening. At any given time during my sessions at schools I was informed of nightmares plaguing youth, severe Post-Traumatic Stress Disorder outcomes, and staff sharing they had no idea how to push through while trying to also heal. It was an onion patch of trauma, and each layer and story was tearfully wrapped in pain.

Alas, somehow and someway our community approached the one year mark after the Fire and many were expressing a soul tired feeling that was all encompassing. The tenacity it had taken to arrive at this stage of recovery left some with a depleted bank of energy, initiative, and sense of hope. It was not getting easier, and for many who shared their truth with me through various projects, it was only getting harder. I was spending each day at the schools and sometimes several schools a day supporting staff and students, and spending every night building the *Phoenix* piece by piece. I was also reaching a euphoric tired, but knew the best parts of my resiliency and impact would be observed by how I chose to model trauma recovery. I knew everyone was watching as I was often on the news for my various projects. In fact, I have been featured on nearly every major national and international news outlet. Yet, regardless if I met with the *New York Times* or a local station, you could find me in paint-covered jeans and a t-shirt, remaining humble to those who gave me a story to tell.

Right before the first anniversary, I was contacted by a local disaster recovery agency. I was asked to take an official role of child life specialist under their wing of support to continue to meet youth on numerous campuses as a counselor. I would travel to numerous schools a week, and be present with a t-shirt that said, "How can I help?" like some sort of Wal-Mart employee. I was so elated to be present again for our community in this chameleon fashion, and it supported my mission to meet humans wherever they were with support. I blended into the ecosystems of each school effortlessly, and was able to serve hundreds of youth.

As the anniversary approached, I buckled down and finished the *Phoenix* in my small apartment. I had received keys everyday since the call for art days after the Fire, and continue to receive keys to this day. I used every key I could by the morning of the first anniversary, packed up the unattached pieces created in my small space, and clicked everything together hours before the reveal. I was so tired it felt like I adopted the exhaustion of everyone I had come in contact with. Yet, I was unworldly motivated to bring my community together. The reveal was first in the day of anniversary events planned for the town. I sat in the building, hearing the roar of a crowd for an hour before one of the biggest days of my life transpired.

I was asked to come outside and greet the crowd, and at the time had not yet looked outside to see how many had gathered for the event. The doors opened and every fiber of my being was humbled by a crowd of thousands that even blocked the main street to just get a peak at my creation. The mayor stood at the podium where I would soon give the soliloquy that provided hope and transparency to all. As the crowd quieted down, penguined together closely in comfort, and sobbed I was awarded the first Key to the Town of Paradise in history. I was gifted this tremendous honor for leading with love, transparency, and humanized help. My biggest take away was a three minute speech I gave to the crowd, news sources, and friends to simply do your part when called to do so within. I encouraged the crowd to celebrate standing tall together one year after they flocked together. I drove home the importance of how we were able to get to this milestone by negating to let barriers of creed, color, age, orientation, and so much more stand in the way. We were one.

Immediately after the reveal, I put my "How can I help?" t-shirt back on and assisted all other events that weekend as a counselor. I have never been so tired and energized at the same time in my life. I continued with the motivation to serve long after the first year and *Phoenix* project. I made more murals with the community, provided more art classes to survivor youth, and led several community capacity building projects. To this day, as we enter the five year mark, I have personally raised over two million dollars through grant writing. Again, highlighting the magic of collaboration which had to exist for any of this to exist. Every conversation and cold call to an administrator or youth organization asking how to help. Listening deeply to what help would, and putting fragmented responses together best I was able to try to respond to those truths. Nothing I did was a solo effort, but a mutual agreement between many who shared the goal of supporting a broken community.

The relationships formed during the first year of my ambitious and out-of-the-box ways of support still linger today. I feel welcome on any school campus in Butte County, and remain close with administrators and teachers. When the pandemic hit, I was thrown into an even more predominant awareness our youth were hurting. I was running a program I created called the "Balanced Brain Project" at a charter school now located in a new town since the Fire. I was teaching about 13 concepts around trauma residue and repair through creative arts expression. I have since implemented this program in over ten schools and have plans of expanding and becoming an evidence-based program of success in the future. I wrote several grants to make this program possible at no burden or cost to the schools and youth organizations served. Another key factor to supporting schools is not to add any stress, financial burden, and extra accountability to the school. I suggest coming with a plan, a timeline, and funding as best you are able when approaching to support anyone after a major disaster. This is easier said than done, but the results will lead to lifelong relationships with mutual benefit to all involved.

At no shock to anyone reading this, the pandemic did not help in the journey of recovery my community was on. In fact, it felt like a clog in the rhythm that was working. The only true thing I have seen and experienced working in regards to healing was the ability to serve people exactly where they were. The pandemic led to thousands who still needed that direct service to become isolated from the resources, support, and social systems bringing them closer to recovery. I chose not to accept this, and knew the outcome of isolation would be just as devastating as the fire for some. I wrote another grant asking for supplies to hand out to my students, and ability to take my program online. I handed out thousands of art kits carefully constructed in my living room. I collaborated with each school when they were handing out educational packets and also gave an art kit to each family. I attached a link to days and times I would offer an art lesson for the items inside. Immediately I was now connected and connecting students from different schools in a new fashion. This program was successful, challenging, and still one of the most embodied examples of the power of collaboration I have seen.

When year four came around, and so many were still isolating in their homes or behind masks, I knew it was time for something new. I then asked for my small Balanced Brain Project to expand with funders I had been blessed by thus far. Before I knew it, the Balanced Brain Project became the new name of several after school programs in Butte County and my curriculum was being adopted and modified to help more youth. Two schools adopted the program, and I opened two after school programs that had never existed that are still running today. This transition taught me my strongest asset is galvanizing and creating innovative approaches to trauma recovery.

I began getting asked to come and lecture about my methods at local schools and universities. I eventually ended up lecturing online to universities around the nation, and have been contracted with the Luther Burbank Center of the Arts to continue sharing how art integration supports trauma. The teaching and lecturing aspect of my strengths were beginning to be more prevalent than before. I realized sharing stories, humanizing help, and using the power of my voice was making an impact for those who also served youth. I now lecture around the nation, and anticipate doing so for a long time and spreading my knowledge to those who will carry it into their journey of support for their communities served. I have contracts with school districts from Santa Rosa to Paradise California and beyond in the virtual realm. I offer professional development training to administrators and teachers in other areas where natural disasters have ravished communities. I plan to continue lecturing, teaching, and tailoring to the needs of communities willing to collaborate.

Atop of the grant writing and program implementations for the first few years, my true self is best viewed when approaching me as an artist first. I love creativity, and personally thrive in it. Yet, I strongly believe and live to prove it is just as much of a tool as an outlet. I have used creative art expression to discuss immensely heavy topics with thousands of people, and it is working. I have received feedback that students are less fidgety after my class, have fewer nightmares, ask for help more, and lessen outbursts when they are confused. The grown-ups have let me know they approach youth more empathetically after I lecture, and that is the greatest win of all. I will continue to teach and preach the power of radical empathy when engaging with your fellow humans. Regardless of trauma, we all simply want to be seen and loved. Youth especially just want to be seen, heard, acknowledged, and supported as the confusion of turbulent feelings races through their underdeveloped brains. We must remember youth are interpreting and learning in a parallel fashion during trauma, and the grown-ups set the tone for how this occurs. When a massive tragedy occurs that has a rippling effect touching every single person in a community for miles, it is hard to name the most balanced person in the room.

The tangled challenge of helping the grown-ups heal alongside youth after a tragedy is monumental but doable. It all boils down to awareness. I teach and model awareness for any and all audiences I influence. I want those who teach to preach, and those who learn to share. The main focuses of my teachings are wrapped closely in the concept that self-awareness, self-care, and vulnerability are the key to recovery. Discovering this by endless exposure to people in pain in Federal Emergency Management Agency camps, basements of airports, camping on pallets in parking lots, college campuses, and resources centers was life changing for me. I have met people wherever they are, however they felt at the time, for nearly five years without skipping a beat.

I took that and evolved it into a career. I now coin myself professionally and personally as a trauma specialist. I am equipped with a very unique and impactful set of skills that aid people in their worst emotional states of mind. I have a gift to sit comfortably with people in harm and provide radical empathy and support. First with the *Phoenix*, then with youth programming, and now serving as a trauma specialist professionally for my community and beyond. I will never take for granted the lessons learned on this journey of selfless surrender. I will never doubt the power of collaboration and creativity. Most importantly I will never forget the thousands of brilliantly broken people who taught me how to teach kindness. I plan to live my life creating, innovating, galvanizing, and implementing trauma recovery programs and techniques. As a kindergartener put it best, I was put on Earth to "make thoughts, things."

CHAPTER 8

PHOENIX RISING

If you have to go through this, call us.
—PUSD Assistant Superintendent David McCready

This chapter provides a summary of the resilience factors individual Paradise Unified School District (PUSD) employees were able to draw on while recovering from the Camp Fire. The PUSD had a great deal going in its favor when tragedy struck, most especially with regard to its personnel. Their humanity and courage inspires hope for all of us. However, the characteristics that made their employees respond to utter devastation in such extraordinary ways might be replicated by other school districts through introspection, dialog, and training. For this reason, readers might consider using this chapter to open a conversation about their own district's strengths and areas for growth.

WHAT IS RESILIENCE?

"Resilience" (as in the *Paradise Resiliency Center*), and its counterpart "strong" (as in *"Paradise Strong"*) have become meaningful and popular terms for expressing unity in recovery in Paradise. These descriptors are ubiquitous in Camp Fire media coverage, and visitors to the Ridge will encounter these words and their variants on signs, bumper stickers, and lapel buttons, and with good reason. Paradise is the epitome of resilient and strong. But what does this actually mean? For the purposes of this book, we define *resilience* broadly as "the process of adapting well in the face of adversity, trauma, tragedy, threats, or even significant sources of stress" (Southwick et al., 2014, p. 1). Resilience factors can be biological, psychological, social, or cultural, and they can be conceptualized as traits, processes, or outcomes. We see all of these in the PUSD: The people we spoke with shared many *traits*, like a sense of humor, a capacity for trust, and a sense of purpose. They engaged in resilience-building *processes* like early and regular preparation for unlikely disasters, long-term, deep engagement with their community, and innovative, out-of-the-box thinking. These manifested resilient *outcomes*, like evacuating thousands of children and teens to safety under unprecedented circumstances, keeping those children and their teachers together in local schools after the disaster, and the eventual rebuilding of many beautifully-designed schools.

FIVE RESILIENCE FACTORS

Resilience Factor One: Preparation

The PUSD took disaster preparation seriously. They created a robust and flexible emergency and evacuation plan that administrators, teachers, and staff reviewed regularly. District employees did not have to figure out what to do when they evacuated their schools; their actions were second nature. Moreover, they understood the spirit of this plan well enough that they were able to improvise when some preestablished procedures were rendered impossible during the Camp Fire. For example, on November 8, their designated "safe zones" for evacuation were also on Fire.

PUSD students also received regular training in wildfire safety. Their teachers were sometimes annoyed at losing instructional time to conduct these in-depth trainings, but they also recognized their importance. Many teachers and administrators grew up in the area, so they understood that the fire risk was real and serious. Training was never just a "hoop" to jump through.

The Camp Fire evacuation taught the PUSD many things that are influencing current planning. Among them:

1. Future evacuation plans need to account for situations where all local evacuation sites are also dangerous. As Camp Fire Educational Coordinator Reiner Light put it, "Nobody has a plan for when your whole town burns down."
2. Future plans should include scenarios for when communications go down. Michelle explained:

In this era you expect to be able to communicate with people. You expect cell phones to work. You expect TV. We had none of that. ...If I had a do-over I would brainstorm with all my leadership team, "What do we do in times when there's no communication?" I would preempt the situation by sending out parent information at the beginning of the year: "In the case of no communication, here's how you get your information."

Resilience Factor Two: Local Understanding and Experience

One of the most important resilience factors buttressing the PUSD's successful response to the disaster was their employees' deep roots in both the Town of Paradise and the school district itself. Many of the teachers, administrators, and staff we interviewed grew up in Paradise, and even those who didn't had very close ties to the community. They viewed Paradise as home, and they wanted to rebuild instead of moving away (moving was often the easier option). Many PUSD employees had worked their way up professionally through various levels in the District, developing expertise in more than one domain. This finding is surprising given that the United States is one of the most geographically mobile countries in the world, and it suggests the professional climate in the PUSD is healthy and supportive enough that people are enticed to remain. As Camp Fire Educational Coordinator Reiner Light (himself a 32-year veteran of the District) explained during his interview, the PUSD is "a good district to stick and stay." Moreover, the perception of Paradise as "home" was an important motivator for PUSD employees to work together toward rebuilding and stabilizing the District: Their recovery efforts were not motivated merely by the desire to get their workplace going again. Instead, they were willing to do anything it took to take care of their "own."

Resilience Factor Three: Creativity

"Everything is figure-outable." This was Tanya Harter's motto for PUSD Food Services, but it beautifully describes an important characteristic of the entire PUSD rescue and recovery story. The day of the Fire, and every day after, brought new, unexpected challenges that had to be met with flexibility, ingenuity, and a willingness to abandon preconceived ideas about how things are "supposed" to be done. The examples are myriad. Consider each of these challenges faced by the PUSD. What would you do?

- You need to evacuate eleven school campuses immediately. Phones and internet are down or only sporadically available, so you can't call parents or emergency services. Repeaters are down, so you cannot communicate with your buses. How do you evacuate the students?

- You decide to put kids in teachers' cars to evacuate them, and to permit them to leave with other people they know. Unfortunately, all the previously established safe zones are also on fire. How do you decide where to send the students?
- You find a safe area outside the Fire zone, and your district drops off hundreds of students and employees. They are hungry, but you have no food. How do you feed them?
- You want to reunite students with their families, but most of their parents' home and cell numbers are not working. How do you connect with families?
- The State says you have to close the District, but your students and their families are begging to come back. Unfortunately you don't have any campuses to receive them. Where do you put your schools? And how long will you take to arrange this?
- Most of your teachers want to come back to work, but you've lost so many students...How do you keep people employed?
- You find some unconventional spaces and create new schools. One of these is a former Facebook building. Another is a hardware store. How do you turn these buildings into functional schools, and how do you get hundreds of homeless kids there every day?
- You've found a way to get the students to their school sites, but all your textbooks and teaching supplies are burned or inaccessible. How do the students spend their days?
- The students need lunch and breakfast, but you don't have your kitchen. How do you feed them?
- The vast majority of your administrators, staff, and students are traumatized. Most have lost their homes and all their possessions. How do you support them going forward?

These questions illustrate some of the system-wide problems that the PUSD had so solve creatively and quickly, but there were dozens, if not hundreds, of other problems requiring creative in-the-moment decision-making by PUSD teachers, administrators, and staff every day. (What do I say to this crying teenager? How do I cover my bus route when I just learned five minutes ago that the insurance adjuster is already at my house? What will I wear to school today, since I lost all my clothes? How do a make this lesson meaningful when all of my students are traumatized?)

Resilience Factor Four: Trust and Mutual Respect

Our interviews make it clear that trust and mutual respect are core values for the PUSD. The superintendents and principals had the utmost faith in their teachers' ability to do their jobs well in the face of seemingly impossible obstacles, so they did not attempt to micromanage. Instead, they asked the teachers what they needed, they moved mountains to see that they got it, and then they stood back and marveled at what the teachers accomplished. The teachers felt this trust, respect, and support, and in turn they trusted and respected their administrators for the daily miracles they were also achieving to keeping the District alive, functional, and often, thriving.

Resilience Factor Five: A Sense of Purpose

The people of Paradise Unified demonstrated selfless regard for their students' wellbeing even at the expense of their own, and even in times of mortal peril. They saved thousands of lives on November 8, 2018, and they continue to do so now in smaller but significant ways every day. They are united in this purpose. The District's Director of Student Services, Dena Kapsalis, encapsulated this beautifully in a story she told during her interview. She first heard it at a professional conference:

> What is our Northern Star here? What is our number one goal? Students. I tell a story to all of our classified staff when I do training on trauma and trauma-informed practices. It's a JFK story about how when he was first elected president he was touring NASA. He saw a guy emptying a trash can behind the building. And he walked up to the guy and asked, "What do you do here?" He was a custodian or a groundskeeper or whatever. But the man's answer was, "I'm sending a man to the moon." The reason why I tell that story to all of our classified staff is to remind them that it doesn't matter where you sit in this organization. You may never see a kid. You may change the oil, you may be a mechanic at the bus yard, or you may be in payroll, or a teacher, or the superintendent, crossing guard, yard duty, bus driver. It doesn't matter where you sit in this organization. You can never forget that you're graduating a kid from high school, that everything you do is in service of that goal. You can't forget that, because that is what we're doing. We are graduating kids from high school.

THE PUSD AS A PHOENIX

Many who have experienced trauma consider the phoenix bird to be an important symbol of resilience. This imagery can be traced to various origins in Greek, Roman, or Egyptian mythology, in which this magical bird dies by fire and is reborn out of the ashes. For the town of Paradise and its PUSD, this image hits very close to home. It is no wonder that Jess Mercer chose this form for her statue, birthing it key by key until all that heartbreak emerged as something poignantly beautiful and new. The PUSD, inclusive of its buildings and its people, is also a phoenix. The people inhabiting these spaces, clearly extraordinary in character before the Fire, emerged from the crucible with new wisdom, empathy, and purpose. It has been our honor to witness this rebirth.

REFERENCE

Southwick, S. M., Bonanno, G. A., Masten, A. S., Panter-Brick, C., & Yehuda, R. (2014). Resilience definitions, theory, and challenges: Interdisciplinary perspectives. *European Journal of Psychotraumatology, 5*, 1. https://doi.org/10.3402/ejpt.v5.25338

EPILOGUE

It's home.
–Jacob Timm, PUSD Director of Facilities, Maintenance, and Operations

The first time I (Amber) visited Paradise after the Fire was just a few weeks after the borders opened. Mom, Dad, and my brother Mike were renting a house in Sacramento, about two hours from town. It was the closest they could get long term given that within a span of four hours about 50,000 people had needed to secure new housing. Dad visited our Paradise property multiple times weekly for cleanup and to supervise the big machines that were hauling away the remnants of everybody's former life. It was very important to him that the workers charged with scraping away the toxic soil spared the concrete sidewalks he had poured himself; these were mostly still intact, and he wanted to build the new house around their borders. Even with his vigilance many of his sidewalks were damaged, and looters managed to steal our mailbox. This had been one of very few salvageable items, so this act hurt more than it should have.

Mom and my brother stayed back in Sacramento during Dad's trips. Mom's dementia had worsened dramatically in the wake of the Fire, and the smoke she inhaled seemed to initiate or exacerbate problems with her lungs and heart. She was now in heart failure and often confused about where they were living. Some days she didn't remember there had been a Fire at all, which is not the win you might think it is. I tell this story because the reader can multiply it many hundreds of times when considering the personal and family challenges faced by the Paradise Unified School District (PUSD), employees who were also caring so well for their students in the days and months after the Fire. The people I interviewed generally alluded to these personal details only in passing, with charming gallows humor, or asked me specifically not to mention how very hard their personal stories were. They wanted to keep the focus on the most important thing—their students.

For many months the water in Paradise was still poisonous. Dad hauled in his own in the back of his newly purchased 2007 Chevy Yukon so he could water the blackened lemon tree and some rose bushes that "might bounce back." Much to the surprise of the rest of us, they did. A few spiders took up residence in the rubble, the first sign that nature does indeed find a way. It would be years before Dad encountered his first squirrel at the feeder he put up, "for anybody left," but they also came back, followed by opossums, skunks, raccoons, and around the four-year anniversary, deer. There was nowhere to purchase food or drinking water in town, so Dad brought his own. He got creative about bathroom breaks. It was hard on him physically, and we worried every time he made the trip. He was nearly 80, and if he hurt himself on the property–still rife with hazard–no one would know unless a demolition worker happened to drive down his gravel road. Truthfully there was no need for Dad to go back so often. So much of the cleanup depended on ever-changing timelines chosen by state officials and Federal Emergency Management Agency, and there was really very little Dad could do on his own. But I also know that he felt he had to make those trips. It was his pilgrimage.

My own first trip to Paradise after the Fire began with a weepy sojourn to see the property, and then as an emotional palate cleanser, a visit to one of the few untouched businesses, a much-loved antiques shop where my Mom and I had spent dozens of hours over the past two decades. Antiquing was always first on our list of things to do when I visited Paradise, and nearly every room of our homes boasted a beautiful or strange treasure, a delicate celadon cup, a vintage pincushion that looked like a mouse, a piece of cake that is actually an oil lamp. Inside the shop it was exactly as it had always been, the smells and textures unchanged. This struck me as intensely poetic; an antique shop is a keeper of things past, and in this context there was something sacred about that. It was as if the shop were a time machine, and I honestly lost myself in the perusal of its wares. But then I would walk by a window. The surrounding terrain was Armageddon. Dozens of burned cars—exactly what you see in the opening scenes of zombie movies—were strewn haphazardly among ruined structures and black remnants of trees. The contrast took my breath away. Blue Murano glass vase. Wasteland. Embroidered tea towel. Devastation. I bought my parents a cheery wooden sign that said, "Paradise is Home," which I thought my Dad would squirrel away for the day he could display it proudly when he moved back. Instead he leaned it against a wall in the living room of the Sacramento rental house, which just made it ironic and sad. Thankfully it has changed locations and now greets guests at their rebuilt home on Esping Way.

Mom, Dad, and my brother Mike moved back to Paradise just before the third anniversary of the Fire, and I visit regularly to see them and breathe in the town. It is still disorienting sometimes because the landmarks keep changing; more often than not the people I interviewed for this book described directions and locations in terms of what "used to be" at a given place. After all, in 2021 the California Department of Finance listed Paradise as the fastest growing city in California. Even as this title falls to others (no doubt Lahaina, Maui will soon be a contender in the state of Hawaii), the landmarks continue to change amid Paradise's re-genesis. The culture has changed, too, it seems to me. There is a rural graciousness and generosity of spirit that I don't remember from before, although some locals tell me it has always been there. I've certainly had many more friendly interactions with random strangers in the supermarket than I ever remember in past visits, and I find people much more willing to assert themselves to be helpful. And it's not necessarily that strangers *say* a lot when you talk with them. In fact they may say very little. There is a shorthand to local communication, as when a surprising snowstorm in March of 2023 excited lots of conversation about past winters. When one Paradise resident said "I had some beautiful photos from a snowstorm in the 1950s" every listener immediately understood how much unarticulated meaning was weighing down that word, "had." "Had" implied she had lost her home, and with it, all their family photos. This shared trauma is omnipresent subtext to every interaction in Paradise, and I think people are kinder because of this mutual understanding.

WHERE ARE THEY NOW?

We began this book with Matt Gates's quiet heroism as he stood in front of his own devastated home and taught us all how to safely sift through Fire debris. As we approach the five-year anniversary of the Camp Fire, the former Paradise Public Information Officer still lives and works in Butte County. He is remarried and has welcomed a new baby to the family. For now, he stays mostly out of the spotlight.

One year after the Camp Fire, Superintendent Michelle John O'Neal sold her home and retired from the PUSD. She shepherded the District through the acute stages of its trauma, and it was time to rest and work on healing her own; three days after the triumphant June 2019 Paradise High School Graduation Ceremony on Om Wraith Field, Michelle's husband Phil John suffered a fatal heart attack while riding his bicycle.[1] Her best friend had also died. Her dog drowned in a pool. The weight of these losses would be staggering even without considering the multiplicative impact of the Camp Fire. Despite all this profound suffering, she has chosen to find joy in active retirement. She adopted a new dog, who she named "Ready" after the Ready Racoon costume Phil donned for Paradise Ridge Fire Safe Council events. On August 13, 2021 she married the dashing Randy O'Neal, and they embarked on a life of adventure. They began with an recreational

---

[1] **The Camp** Fire had lasting consequences, among them stress-related illness. Many Paradise residents assert that the Fire has yet to claim it's last victims.

vehicle trip around the United States before settling into a beautiful new home out of state. She has since welcomed her fourth grandchild, and often visits and hosts her adult children. She is happy. When I asked her about this, here is what she said:

> You know what, I still am sad every single day. I'll be very honest. I'm still sad every single day. I'm still pissed off, you know, a little bit. But I'm also very happy. And I have to move on. Because that's what you have to do in life. So I'm sad that this happened to us. And—And when I say "pissed off" I still have some anger towards PG&E. I'll admit it… But you know what? It's done. It's done, so now we have to move forward.

Michelle and the other two legs in the Three-Legged Stool remain very close. She talks with Superintendent Tom Taylor and Assistant Superintendent David McCready at least once per week. In these conversations she sometimes weighs in on high-level decisions or simply admires Tom and David's approach to PUSD leadership. But the laughter they cultivated during the very worst of times remains vital to their relationship:

> We talk once a week at least. We get on FaceTime, all three of us, and we do this: [She uses three fingers to imitate a stool with three legs.] We do this all the time. And then they kick me out and do this: [She demonstrates the stool tipping over because it only has two legs now. This is accompanied by laughter and the sound of the stool tipping over – "aaaaah"]. So we're still very close, all three of us. We'll never be not very close. We went through hell and back with each other.

Tom Taylor and David McCready remain a powerhouse administrative team, navigating typical District leadership responsibilities while essentially re-imagining and manifesting a brand new architectural and pedagogical footprint for an entire District. In August of 2023 they shared their excitement at the public Grand Opening of Paradise High School, but behind closed doors they are bonded in ways that most of us will never understand:

> *Tom:* It's kind of weird. I mean we've always worked really well together, but after the Fire he and I walked out of the town together…Now I would definitely say we are more than just colleagues.
> *David:* Yes.
> *Tom:* Definitely friends. Everybody would think that David and I are best friends. [laughing]…It's kind of funny. [both smiling] We're not near as tense with each other as we—not that we were ever tense, but we're a whole lot more loose when we're together than we used to be. [laughing].

When I asked Tom what he hoped readers of this book might take away from the PUSD's Camp Fire story, he said this:

> I think it's an incredible story about how a community came together over horrible circumstances to support one another. And really I don't want to say, "come out of it", because we're not out of it yet. I mean, all you've got to do is look around and see that there is so much to be done. But what I hope is that people see [this story] as a community that came together.

Prior to the Fire, Reiner Light had been planning on retiring from his principal position at Paradise Intermediate School. When he was asked to take on the new role of Camp Fire Educational Coordinator, he chose to stay on with PUSD. While technically retired now, he maintains ties with the District and works for them on an as-needed basis. He stayed on, he says, because of the people. During his interview, he mentioned his "highest respect" for Tom Taylor and David McCready, both for their past and current leadership of PUSD, but also for their daring actions the morning of the fire:

> Let me let me just say it is nothing short of heroic. What they did to make sure that the schools were all okay, and the town is burning down around them. Absolutely incredible. That's why I still do my job. I'm just like, "if you guys need something—You guys are the reason why Paradise Unified is still here".

When I asked Reiner to describe his current life, he said he didn't think about the Fire much anymore, except when he drives up to Paradise for work or to check on the plot of land where his house used to be. "There are times," he says, when he thinks about his former life, but he considers himself very fortunate on several counts. First, within two weeks of the fire he and his wife Tina were in escrow on new home in neighboring Chico. (Tina took on all the insurance and housing responsibilities making Reiner's work for PUSD possible.) Second, they have two grandchildren and two bulldogs to keep them busy. The grandchildren weren't visiting during our interview, but the dogs, Chloe and Claire, were by his side. "Chloe's tongue is just a little oversized," he shows me. "Hangs out most of the time." He pats her, and then gives her sister a good rub. "So, you know," he says, "life is good."

Jacob Timm is still the PUSD Director of Facilities, Maintenance, and Operations. After the Fire his family also relocated to Chico, but urban life was never a comfortable fit. He was itching to get back. "Paradise," he told me, "It's home." In 2021 his family purchased their "forever home" in their former neighborhood. His son Hunter graduated from Paradise High in 2022. Jake still works very long hours, but in his off-time he can be found on the sidelines of Paradise High School football games, or riding his motorcycle with family and friends in the beautiful Sierra foothills.

Dena Kapsalis is still providing services to students and families as the Director of Student Services in Paradise Unified School District. Her previous school, Honey Run Academy, has not yet been rebuilt. Her Student Services team continues to provide support, resources, access, and equity to all students in Paradise Unified. These include support and resources for Homeless and Foster youth, community outreach for chronically absent students, Special Education support, alternative placements and any other obstacles that might get in the path of student success. Dena's youngest child graduated from high school in 2022 and is attending college in Boston. Her oldest is also in college in Chicago. Dena and her husband spend a lot of time in Chicago and Boston - which is a great perk of having kids in those cities! Dena and her family continue to live by the credo: Think Fast and Live Slow.

Paradise Intermediate School principal Larry Johnson lived in Chico at the time of the Fire, so he did not need to relocate. However, his mother lost the home he was raised in, and she has since moved to Chico as well. When I interviewed Larry in early 2023, Paradise Intermediate School (PINT) had long-since relocated from the Orchard Supply Hardware. He guided it through a temporary transition to the Paradise High School campus, then to online learning and hybrid instruction during Covid-19. When everyone returned to campus in 2021, the District renamed PINT "Paradise Junior High School (PJHS)." In 2022 PJHS shut down approximately two-thirds of its classrooms and the physical education/lunchtime field for construction renovations. During this year Larry's PJHS office was closet-sized and he shared one wall with a staff bathroom. He ironically explained that hearing the toilet flushing was "a treat," but he was sincere in his appreciation for what he had: "It's not in an aisle. It's not at a mall!" A few months before the fifth anniversary of the Fire he moved into a new, spacious office with an "amazing view" of the green lawn in the front of the school. "The students have the campus back," he wrote in an email to me, "we are able to spread out and have full use of the space."

Larry's Orchard Supply Hardware teachers, Cynthia Smith and Tracy Parks, continue to work for the district. Cynthia still teaches seventh and eighth-grade science at Paradise Junior High, and is grateful to finally be living back in town. Her new home is large and comfortable, and living so close to work after many years of commuting has provided some relief. Her children are growing up in the Paradise schools. She finally feels stability, despite her hectic teaching schedule of 180 students. Four years after the fire she took her first summer off, and she spent part of that time in Greece with her daughter. Tracy Parks still lives 50 minutes from Paradise in her dear friends' granny unit, and describes her life now as "simpler and more fun" than it was in previous years. Her children have adjusted well to their new situation, and she enjoys working with students through PUSD's Elearning academy.

Paradise Elementary fourth-grade teacher Victoria Steindorf became Tracy's partner in Paradise Elearning for a few years, but she reluctantly retired in 2022. Not long before the Fire Victoria received a cancer diagnosis, and ultimately had to have one of her lungs removed. This did not deter her; she kept teaching until she caught Covid from some students—a particularly scary experience for someone with only one lung. These days you can sometimes find her smiling at you from behind a fruit and vegetable stand called "Julia's," mountain biking on local trails, or just loving on her dog Rainie and husband, Dave.

Our wonderful Lunch Ladies, Tanya Harter and Linda Shields, still feed about 2,500 Paradise children and teens every day. Tanya continues to head her department as PUSD Director of Food Services. Her office has yet to be rebuilt, but she says she's not worried about that. She is making do with her "little niche of a space." (Recall that her mantra is "everything is figure-outable"). When asked why she keeps coming to work every day she responded, "I guess I want to see how it all turns out. I want to see my last [lunch lady] who is still in a trailer get her house." Either way, she plans on staying with PUSD until she retires. She is proud of her team's tenacity:

> There are a few of us directors who were here prior [to the Fire] and who are still doing our jobs. We're still here. And there are so many principals that can't say that. So we're like this little group of survivors, you know, folks who still come to work every day, regardless of what the world of Paradise throws at us.

Linda works as Food Services Site Manager at Paradise High School. The Camp Fire spared her home, but there are scars. Echoes of those seven days when she did not know where her husband or son were, remain. Counseling sessions helped, she says, but "you know, if the phone goes out, you kind of—just-your body just freaks out. Mine did anyway." When I pointed out to her how impressed I was that she stuck it out and stayed with the District, she responded, "Yes. Yes. Because this is home."

Angie Van Blaricom, the bus driver "last off the hill" on November 8, 2018, still lives on the Ridge and continues to drive a special needs bus for PUSD. When I asked her how it feels to retrace her most harrowing route each day, she was sanguine:

> It doesn't traumatize me. It's memories, you know. I still go by that stop every day of my life. I'm on that road driving different kids, but they come down that road. I deliver children to Ponderosa like I did back in the day. It's not the same, because we used to pull into the school. Now we pull up next to the school to drop them off. So things have changed, it's a memory that'll never go away. But it can't control you. Life goes on, you know.

Chris Rinesmith still trains bus drivers and drives buses for the PUSD. She and her husband live in their pre-Fire home in Magalia. This has provided constancy as they near retirement, and it has been "healing" for her to stay in the area and be part of the recovery process. However, her long-term plans have been disrupted by the economic injury of having lost three underinsured rental properties which were part of her retirement financial planning. Nevertheless, she maintains her sense of adventure. In 2023 she traveled to Japan to welcome her 11th grandchild, a beautiful little boy named Cyrus.

Jess Mercer still resides in Butte County, and has expanded her work to include neighboring areas. In the years since the Fire she has created over 100 community-oriented therapeutic art collaborations and contributions, generating more than a million dollars in funding for the Ridge. In 2022 she celebrated the grand opening of an important initiative, the Equilibrium Community Wellness Center, in Paradise. This recreational space aims to "broaden the scope of resilience, recovery, and healing" by providing a venue for Ridge residents to gather, seek community, and recreate in the historical, etymological sense of the word—to *re-create* themselves in times of stress. More recently she's turned her attention to teaching other people how to do construction. This is understandably a much-needed skill set in the Fire scar. She continues to make art for her own mental health, and to share this love of art with her community. She married her wife, Ashley, in 2021. She's feeling more settled now, quieter of spirit, I think, and savoring domestic life with Ashley, their dog Mollie, and their cat, Monte.

APPENDIX A: ADVICE FROM OUR EXPERTS

When we pitched this book to the Paradise Unified School District (PUSD) employees we hoped to interview, the clincher for many was the opportunity to offer guidance to other teachers, administrators, counselors, and school staff who might someday face a similar disaster. They were so eager to help. Here is what they had to say.

ADVICE FROM THE SUPERINTENDENTS

Michelle John O'Neal

Before the disaster

- Don't take your situation for granted. Life can change in an instant.
- Take time now to build resilience skills.
- Make sure your disaster preparedness plan is up to date.
- Prepare regularly during your leadership team meetings. Really "drill down": What are you going to do if X, Y, Z happens? Consider multiple scenarios. What if your plan A isn't possible? What if Plan B isn't possible?
- Plan alternative means of communication. Keep your old-fashioned phone tree triage.

After the disaster

- Don't react immediately. Wait, talk with others, and respond with thoughtfulness.
- Walk beside your team. There is no need to walk in front of them. Use your leadership team. Remember that superintendents are not "the end-all." You do not have to make all the decisions.

- Remember that people have a need to give, but they don't always know what you need until you ask.
- Take care of yourself. Ask for help. You are no good to anyone if you are "curled up in a ball somewhere."
- You don't always have to be the "super person." It's okay to let others see you cry.

Tom Taylor and David McCready

- Make sure you have a plan for reuniting students and their parents after a disaster. Keep it simple. Make sure everyone, including parents, knows the plan. Publish it. Practice.
- Verify that your reuniting plan includes locations in neighboring cities or towns in case none of the local choices are safe.
- When you need something, ask for it. It's okay to push for what you need. Other districts and groups will help you.
- Sometimes you need to bend the rules in extreme circumstances. (e.g. normally no district would place a school near an airport, but PUSD did.)

ADVICE FROM THE DIRECTOR OF FACILITIES, MAINTENANCE AND OPERATIONS

Jacob Timm

- Digitize everything you can and save it on the Cloud. (Paradise lost hard copies of all their inspection reports and building plans for all their schools. Some of these were old historic sites that were not saved digitally elsewhere.)
- People can feel a wonderful sense of purpose centered around what still remains after the disaster. Take time to notice what you still have.
- Prioritize getting any remaining school sites up and running. These spaces can offer a much-needed sense of normalcy for the students.
- Create systems for the disaster cleanup. Be strategic.
- Understand that maintenance is different when you are dealing with landlords at new sites.
- Be ready with Go Bags.
- Be prepared for the unexpected. Every day will bring new challenges.
- Try not to take things personally.

ADVICE FROM THE CAMP FIRE EDUCATIONAL COORDINATOR

Reiner Light

- Believe in your people. They will amaze you.
- Trust your people to take initiative during and after the disaster. Prepare and practice so they are equipped to do so. If you are not available because of the incident, they need to be able to step in and take control.
- Ask your teams what they need. Empower them to act. Make sure they report back to you.
- Communication is everything. Keep the lines open.
- Practice specific scenarios to develop flexible and quick thinking when the real thing happens. For example, "you've got 10 people and you're stranded on Mars. What do you do first?" or "There's been a big hurricane, and three quarters of your town has been washed out to sea. What do you do now?"
- Maintain several hard copies of your disaster plans and current student contact information. Computers may go down, and you may not have time to print anything.
- Remember that every staff member's home situation is different. For example, some have a spouse who can handle insurance claims, finding new housing, etc., whereas others are doing all of this on their own. Some staff members may find themselves suddenly commuting long distances and not have money for gas. The disaster situation is difficult for everyone, but more difficult for some.
- Recognize and acknowledge (out loud) the work people are doing. Tell them when they are amazing. Buy them lunch.

Handling donations

- Appoint someone in advance who will be the organizer of donations, should a disaster occur.
- Develop a process to handle donations. Keep thorough records of cash and gift card donations and follow the law. This part, by itself, can feel overwhelming.
- Report donations to your School Board. Make sure they approve how it is allocated.
- Someone will have to receive and record the donations. That same person should also write the "Thank You" letters. If possible, other people will need to deliver them to the schools. Plan who will do these things.

- You will probably need to dedicate a large space to store donations of goods.
- Some well-meaning people will donate things that are not useful (e.g. used books from their home library). Others will earmark donations for specific schools or groups. Have a plan for dealing with this. It is okay to say "Thank you, but we don't need this" or put a sign on the door "No more backpacks please."

ADVICE FROM THE PRINCIPAL

Larry Johnson

- Spend money, and do it early. Administrators are naturally frugal and cautious about this, but in a disaster situation *funds are going to come in*, from the government, from insurance, from grants and donations. Speed up recovery by making sure teachers have what they need. If necessary, authorize them to buy what they need and save documentation for reimbursement.
- Delegate, trust your people, and support them even if it doesn't go perfectly.
- You don't just lead when you want to. You lead when you're needed.
- Prioritize the social and emotional domains when dealing with students. Academics provide the structure, but they are not the first priority.
- Teachers are your front-line emotional support for each other and for the students. They will be there for each other, to give hugs, tell a joke, or let someone cry.

ADVICE FROM THE DIRECTOR OF STUDENT SERVICES

Dena Kapsalis

- When dealing with other people in a disaster situation, assume strength and not fragility. Assume strength for yourself also.
- Understand that there are predictable patterns of behavior when disasters occur. There is a literature on this. Consider reading Schonfeld, D., Lichtenstein, R., Kline Pruett, M., & Speese-Linehan, D. (2002). *How to prepare and respond to a crisis.* Association for Supervision and Curriculum Development, & Solnit, R. (2009). *A paradise built in hell: The extraordinary communities that arise in disaster.* Penguin.

- Keep in mind that disasters expose previous inequalities. Students with fewer resources before a disaster are likely to experience more disruption afterward.
- Support services do not help if students and families cannot access them. Keep a focus on transportation.
- A message to colleagues in other school districts: Think before you send emails or messages that require a response. Employees at the impacted sites will be dealing with hundreds of messages and they are overwhelmed.
- Avoid donation fatigue by appointing an outside person to coordinate donations and figure out where to store donated items. Keep this off the plate of school personnel in the impacted District. Consider appointing this person ahead of time as part of your planning.
- Appoint a School Recovery Coordinator. This person can coordinate services for school employees and students and identify alternative locations for these services. This will free up school staff to focus on doing the jobs they are trained to do.
- Be aware of compassion fatigue. Take care of yourself.
- Appoint a committee to vet the legitimacy of organizations that offer help. Some of these are wonderful; others are predatory. These want to sell you services or bill you for "free" help.
- Expect some conflict within your district. This is normal after a disaster. Plan how you might respond organizationally.
- Be flexible and creative in decision-making. It's okay to do things very different than before.

ADVICE FROM THE TEACHERS

Tracy Parks

- Long after media attention wanes and people turn their attention to other disasters, people will still be struggling. Recovery is an ongoing process.
- Prioritize students' social and emotional needs. Learning can't happen when they are dysregulated.
- Get comfortable with imperfection. Think: "It is what it is, and we'll be normal later."
- Know that our number one job is to be the best you can be for the kids. Your attitude is contagious.
- Make your classroom a safe space for socializing before and after school. Let it bring scattered people together.

- Get creative with your classroom environment and use the circumstances. Use your weird setting as part of your assignments (e.g. what cool pedagogical things could you do in an empty hardware store that you couldn't do in your classroom?).
- You may notice a sense of entitlement emerges in the students at some point after the disaster. Their parents may have indulged them because they lost so much, and they may have a hard time adjusting to more rigorous academics as things get closer to "normal" at school.

Cynthia Smith

- Students are more willing to open up when they are active. Check in emotionally while walking from place to place.
- Remember that parents in disaster situations are often just as stressed out and depressed as their children are. Be understanding, and don't let academic expectations add more pressure.
- Let go of all the academic "shoulds," as in "they should be learning X or Y." Prioritize social and emotional needs. You can do this and still learn academics. For example, for a middle school science lesson Cynthia let the students create Christmas cards using paper circuits.

Victoria Steindorf

- Remember that after a disaster, staff may not have money for gas to get to work. They need the job, but they can't afford to work.
- Expect that teachers might feel that allocation of post-disaster resources or privileges is unfair to them or their school, Try to make it fair.
- Consider starting each day with a checklist for your traumatized students. Example items include "I feel like I need to see a counselor," "I need to sit by myself today," or "I need to say hi to my mom." You can't just start the day, with "Open your book to page 45."
- It is healing to be in a classroom with others who shared the disaster experience.
- Structure and routine help tremendously, even if those routines are different.
- Focus on the positive, and seek out people who do the same. You can't think about the sadness all the time.
- You may have more porous boundaries with students. It's okay to share a bit more than you previously would have. You can say I love you. You can give hugs. This is a "different vulnerability" than normal.

ADVICE FROM THE BUS DRIVER/TRAINER AND BUS DRIVER

Chris Rinesmith

- Equip buses with N95 masks or something that is able to filter smoke. Make sure there are both adult and child-sized masks. Store them in waterproof packaging. Some PUSD bus drivers had to improvise and make masks out of clothing.
- Store water (and maybe emergency snacks) on buses. Some PUSD students were stuck on buses for hours trying to get out of town. They were very thirsty.
- Designate someone to stay in communication with all the buses while they are evacuating. (Caveat 1: This person isn't in the field, so they will have a different perspective than the drivers who are actually on the road. Caveat 2: Phones and two-way radios went down during the evacuation, so after a certain time period this would not have helped in Paradise.)
- After the disaster, recognize when you need a break. Take "a step back" when you need to.
- Keep good habits. Get enough sleep. Eat well. Have lunch with friends. Laugh. Go out on the weekend.
- Don't sweat the small stuff when it comes to discipline. That rowdy kid just lost their house.

Angie Van Blaricom

- It's difficult to plan for something you've never experienced, so stay observant. Look at what's going on around you, and stay calm.
- Don't rely on gut feelings. Firefighters don't rely on gut feelings either. They plan, they look, and they know what's going on around them. Do that.
- Be loving and supportive of the kids on your bus, but be firm. You are not their friend. You are an adult.

ADVICE FROM THE FOOD SERVICE DIRECTORS

Tanya Harter

- Tap into folks who have been there. Call Paradise.
- Tap into your local folks. Even people who haven't "been there" can show extraordinary insight and resourcefulness.

- Remember that everything, absolutely everything, is "figure-outable." Maybe put a sign over your workspace that reminds you of this.
- Appreciate the good days, when everything goes smoothly and as planned. Take time to notice when this happens.
- Acknowledge the positives. (PUSD gained some wonderful new employees after the Fire.)

Linda Shields

- Take every day as a new experience because things will not be the same as yesterday.
- Helping the students can help you. Giving them the stability of a nice lunch can help with your own trauma. Helping others is good for your soul.
- Lunchtime can feel very "normal" when everything else is so strange. Students really appreciate this. They give hugs and say "thank you so much!"
- Lean on your colleagues. Take time to talk with them and share experiences.
- A great supervisor can make all the difference. Three things that really helped us were (1) her flexibility, (2) she cared about us, and (3) she "researched every possibility" to help us feed the children.
- Consider writing up a food service disaster plan.

APPENDIX B: SELECTED RESOURCES

BOOKS

Nonfiction Books About the Camp Fire

Gale, D., & Rodriguez, A. (2023). *Sifting through the ashes: Finding beauty, peace, love, and strength through trauma.* DGC Publishing.

Gee, A., & Anguiano, D. (2021). *Fire in Paradise: An American tragedy.* WW Norton & Co.

Johnson, L. (2021). *Paradise: One town's struggle to survive an American wildfire.* Crown.

Maxwell, K. (2023). *Snow after fire: A memoir of the Paradise camp fire and its aftermath.* Legacy Book Press.

Plaschke, B. (2021). *Paradise found: A high school football team's rise from the ashes.* HarperCollins.

"Coffee Table" Books

Keister, D. (2019). *People, places and pieces of Paradise: The inferno, aftermath & recovery of the most destructive wildfire in California history.* Douglas Keister Photography.

Midling, P., Schwager, R., & Ballou, C. (2019). *The California camp fire: Reflections and remnants.* Independently Published.

Moore, D. J., Grammer, S., & Campbell, D. (2021). *Beauty among the ashes: An artist's quest to bring hope to a town that lost everything.* Independently published.

Nonfiction History Books About Paradise

Colby, R. (2006). *Images of America: Paradise.* Arcadia.

Reifschneider-Smith, J. (2019). *Tales of the Paradise ridge.* Association for Northern California Historical Research in Cooperation with the Paradise Gold Nugget Museum.

Fiction Books About the Camp Fire

Brown, S. D., & Peters, S. (2019). *I escaped the California camp fire*. Best Day Books. (For readers nine and up).
Hosmer, K. M. (2018). *Barclay's big adventure*. CreateSpace, a Division of Amazon.
Tarshis, L. (2020). *I survived the California wildfires, 2018*. Scholastic. (For grades 2-7).

Poetry About the Camp Fire

Hartley, B. (2019). *Fire on the ridge: A collection of poems by Bill Hartley*. Gold Dust Press.
Henson, J. R. (2019). *The camp fire: Dreams, nightmares, hopes*. Independently published.
Rosales, M., Knittel, P., Janke, S., & Harding, C. (2021). *Voices of Paradise: Before the fire took our town-selections from a writers group in Paradise California*. Independently published.

FILMS ABOUT THE CAMP FIRE

Canepari, Z., & Cooper, D. (Directors). (2019). *Fire in Paradise* [Film]. Netflix Studios.
Durán, E. (Directors). (2020). *All its name implies: Fire, ash, and the resilience of Paradise*. U.T.B. Studios.
Greengrass, P. (Directors). (2025). *The lost bus* [Film]. Blumhouse Productions and Apple Original Films.
Howard, R. (Directors). (2020). *Rebuilding Paradise* [Film]. National Geographic.
Kessler, T. (Directors). (2019). *From the ashes: A Paradise school documentary* [Short Film]. Tava Kessler.
McMullen, J. (Directors). (2019). *Frontline: Fire in Paradise* [Season 2019, Episode 16]. WGBH.
Parsons, K. (Directors). (2021). *The fire cats: Save something small* [Film]. Ravenshoe Media.
Vinson, J. (Directors). (2022). *Paradise strong: Surviving California's deadliest wildfire* [Film]. V Squared Media.
Walker, L. (Directors). (2021). *Bring your own brigade* [Film]. Paramount.
Wolfe, C. (Executive Producer). (2020). *This old house*. (Season 41, Episodes 15 and 16). This Old House Ventures, LLC.

SELECTED WEBSITES

(Many of these organizations also maintain social media pages, which may offer different information.)

- *Camp Fire Collaborative:* https://www.campfire-collaborative.org/

Appendix B: Selected Resources ▪ 137

- *Camp Fire Survivors:* CampFireSurvivors.com
- *Make it Paradise:* https://makeitparadise.org/
- *Paradise Unified School District:* https://www.pusdk12.org/
- *Paradise Ridge Chamber of Commerce:* https://www.paradisechamber.com/
- *Rebuild Paradise Foundation:* https://www.rebuildparadise.org/
- *Regenerating Paradise:* https://www.regeneratingparadise.org/
- *Town of Paradise:* https://www.townofparadise.com/

www.ingramcontent.com/pod-product-compliance
Lightning Source LLC
Chambersburg PA
CBHW050539300426
44113CB00012B/2177